PRAISE FOR DEFIN

"When I began reading *Define Your Why*, I was pulled in by Barbara's personal stories. When I reached Chapter 6, 'find your ikigai,' I was struck that deep personal reflection work pushes readers to think and feel in ways that expand our understanding of concepts of self and connections to others. In reading this chapter, it became evident that living inside our vulnerability is essential to growing who we are socially and emotionally. It's an SEL curriculum for adults!"
—**Dr. Pam Moran**, co-author *Timeless Learning* and Executive Director of the Virginia School Consortium of Learning

"More than ever, educators need to refuel their passion for teaching and learning but don't have a plan of action. *Define Your Why* provides that spark to ignite even those who are burnt out. This book also goes the extra mile and provides a blueprint with inspirational stories, calls to action, and models to ensure one's passion for teaching doesn't extinguish."
—**Shelly Sanchez Terrell**, Author: *30 Goals Challenge for Teachers* and *Small Steps to Transform Your Teaching and Learning to Go* Founder: #Edchat, 30Goals.com, @EdspeakersCo

"With her trademark warmth and authenticity, Barbara shares her own personal journey that took her from 'dental flossing to mental flossing.' Along with the insights she has gained from forging her own path as an educator, coach, and edupreneur, Barbara will provide you with many practical tools to help you find your own ikigai ("reason for being") and more importantly to move from "me to we" as you help your learners discover theirs.

Excerpts from interviews with a number of experts in the field (Barbara is the ultimate connector) provide a variety of rich perspectives on the topics discussed in the book. The book comes at an important time. Decades of a negative narrative have left many educators wondering why they do what they do - this book is a great way to get reoriented to the passion and commitment to equity that brought you into education in the first place. I highly recommend it, especially to educators who are just getting started in their careers."

—**Luis F. Pérez**, Author: *Learning on the Go* (CAST) & *Dive into UDL* (ISTE). Technical Assistance Specialist, National AEM Center at CAST, ISTE Inclusive Learning Network

"When I think about the educators who made the deepest impression in my life, wonderful memories of men and women who were passionate about teaching and who took a personal interest in my learning come to mind immediately. They had a great sense of humor, and they pushed me when they knew they could but were there to never let me fail. In reading Barbara Bray's book, Define Your Why, I have finally realized why these educators were so impressionable. Barbara shares her insightful journey through her childhood and adult learning and, through that reflection, creates opportunities for you personally to dig deep into who you are and to then challenge you to bring it into your classroom strategies.

Barbara creates your backpack for this journey, allowing you to pack it with your particular assets and talents and allows you to be open to those things that challenge you. The many activities she describes are engaging for both you and your students to Define their Why. From there, the journey through designing personalized learning experiences is at your fingertips. I know you will find Define Your Why will be inspirational, educational, and a wealth of new knowledge about yourself and your learners."

—**Rose Colby,** Competency Education Specialist, Consultant, Author of *Competency-Based Education: The New Architecture for K-12 Schooling*

"Barbara Bray is as wonderful a storyteller in writing as she is in person. This book will inspire readers to discover their why."
—**Nancy Weinstein**, co-founder and CEO of MindPrint Learning, and co-author *The Empowered Student*

"If you are struggling to discover your WHY, you must read Barbara Bray's new book. Through powerful storytelling, practical advice, and personal self-discovery activities, DEFINE YOUR WHY provides the blueprint to figure out what you were put on this earth to do! Each of us deserves to live our lives with PURPOSE, and this book needs to be the start of your journey. Discover your WHY, embrace it, and share it so that others know exactly what you are bringing to the world!"
—**Rich Czyz**, proud principal and learner, co-founder of 4 O'Clock Faculty #4OCF, author of *The Four O'Clock Faculty* and *The Secret Sauce*

Published by EduMatch®
PO Box 150324, Alexandria, VA 22315
www.edumatchpublishing.com

ISBN: 978-1-970133-46-2

DEFINE YOUR WHY

OWN YOUR STORY SO YOU CAN LIVE & LEARN
ON PURPOSE

BARBARA BRAY

EduMatch Publishing

CONTENTS

This book is dedicated to the love of my life,
my husband, who stole my heart
the first time I met him.

Tom, thank you for being my best friend
with me along my journey
to define my WHY!

MY WHY FOR THIS BOOK

> *It's not enough to have lived. We should be determined to live for something."*

— WINSTON S. CHURCHILL

My WHY for writing this book was because I realized how challenging it was to teach, how difficult it was to be a student, and how many educators have gotten lost in the WHAT and HOW that they've forgotten or maybe never knew their WHY. This is a book for anyone who wants to discover or re-discover their WHY. I've spent most of my life as a teacher, a coach, and a mentor supporting teachers and administrators. Something is different now. I feel there is a sense of urgency to rethink the idea of "school" and what it means to be a teacher, a principal, and a student. I have also heard from others outside of education who felt lost and didn't know their WHY. They said they accepted that they went down the wrong path and felt they were living someone else's story. This made me stop and rethink my WHY. I became aware that that had happened to me. I thought I had no other choice, but I did. This book is all about the stories of how I discovered my purpose and how others discovered theirs. Just like

Winston Churchill's quote above, "we should be determined to live for something."

Do you ever feel like you are going through the motions just to get through the day? You may have a job, children, parents, or other people or things you may be responsible for. You continue to do what you have to do every day because you have always done it that way. You may not have even considered that you could do anything different. Consider if any of the following "what ifs" resonates with you. **What if you...**

- are treated fairly in your job and feel appreciated?
- have a job that pays you enough that you are valued and not stressed about your bills?
- as a teacher, have the support, resources, and time to do what you need and want to do?
- as an administrator, have people on board for the change that needs to happen?
- as a student, focus on what you would love to learn, instead of tests and grades?
- as a parent, don't have to worry about your kids' choices?
- are retired and excited about your plans for the rest of your life?
- are living life and enjoying each moment as it happens?

There can be many more things that impact you and your thoughts. I wanted you to think about your "what ifs" positively instead of going to the negative. Change can be difficult. What is keeping you from changing what you do or from finding time to consider who you are, what your passions are, and why you are here? There are many things that can impact your life. Your day-to-day routines or just being concerned about having to change may keep you from becoming your best YOU.

Over the past few years, I have heard from many people who have concerns about their lives, their jobs, and from some who have not been sure how to change what they do even when they are really unhappy in their current situations.

What if you take time to pause and think about your WHY?

I wrote this book around the process I went through to figure out my own WHY. I have been thinking about my purpose and my WHY for as long as I can remember. I've had my own reservations and been cautious about changing or doing something new. I've asked myself loads of questions and, in the process, learned about me. I used this process to coach others. I've worked with educators, parents, students, family, and friends who told me that they were frustrated with what they were doing, who they thought they were, and some have told me that they were ready to give up. Many of their stories made me sad and, for some, I was even scared for them. I learned strategies that helped guide the process to help them find their why. I want to share that process with you. I really believe that when you know your WHY and you have the strategies you need to believe in yourself, you will find a way to live and learn on purpose.

The process works since it is personal for you because it is about YOU. Yes, I'll ask you some difficult questions that will make you think deeply, do some things that may be uncomfortable, but I hope you end up relieved and excited to find the real YOU. A few questions to digest as you start this book:

- Has anyone ever asked you why you are here?
- Have you asked yourself what is your purpose and meaning for life?
- What if everyone started addressing their WHY right now?

You're probably thinking that working on these questions is not possible because you have things that have to be done first. Let's address PURPOSE. Let's think of a baby's purpose. It is about surviving and being loved and cared for; all necessary for a baby to live. Yet, have you thought that an important purpose for a baby is to be curious. Just watch a baby find their hands for the first time. Curiosity pushes a baby to want to crawl and then walk. Curiosity pushes all of us to want to learn. What I want to address is the importance of knowing your purpose now but realize that your purpose may be one thing at one time in your life, and then it changes with all the different experiences you have throughout your life.

<u>Your WHY changes as you grow and learn.</u>

The steps to find and define your WHY involve multiple activities that can help you learn more about you and guide you to explore your passions. Each chapter provides stories, ideas, tips, and questions along with why you need to know your WHY now. You can start at the beginning or jump to any chapter that resonates with you. Use this book as your guide as you go on your journey to discover your WHY and to own and tell your story.

What is in this book and WHY

Each chapter folds and weaves in quotes, activities, links, QR codes, questions to ponder, wonderings, resources, and personal stories from me and 26 inspirational educators and thought leaders. The companion website is linked from Barbara's website at https:// barbarabray.net and digital resources and downloadable charts for the activities you can use as you read this book are at http://bit.ly/ defineyourwhy-digital.

Chapter 1: WHY Share Your Backstory?

All of us are impacted by experiences, people, and decisions that happened in our past. This chapter is about my backstory. I share how different events and experiences impacted who I am today and how your own backstory may have impacted you and others. The activities and questions in this chapter will guide you to build your backstory and an event chart that you can refer to later.

Chapter 2: WHY Be the Main Character of Your Story?

There is no one like you in the whole world. You know *you* better than anyone else. Even though you know you, you may not know some important things about you. This chapter has you as the main character of your story and how to build your story around you. Starting with the characteristics of a character in a story you read, you will then consider what qualities describe you best, then you can build YOU as the main character of your own story.

Chapter 3: WHY Start with your WHY?

This chapter reviews Simon Sinek's Golden Circle and why we need to start with our WHY. Most of us grew up being told what to do and how to learn. We learned to be compliant and didn't ask WHY we were doing or learning something. Through different WHY stories and activities, you will be able to start with your WHY, determine if it is aligned to your WHAT, and create your draft WHY statement.

Chapter 4: WHY Go with your Strengths, Skills, and Dispositions?

This chapter addresses how you find the strengths beyond your talents to identify your current skills and dispositions, your skills gap, and what you may need for your future. We will discuss the future of work and the Industrial Revolutions, and what that means about job loss and the importance of upskilling. We will address your mindset, aspirations, and any self-doubts you may have.

Chapter 5: WHY use Universal Design for Learning?

In this chapter, you will be introduced to Universal Design for Learning (UDL) and why it starts with the WHY of learning. You will explore the framework of the UDL Guidelines and checkpoints to discover your strengths, competencies, challenges, and obstacles. With this information, you can then design your Learner Profile and build your Personal Learning Backpack with tools, apps, learning strategies, skills, and competencies.

Chapter 6: WHY Find your ikigai?

This chapter will share *ikigai* as the Japanese concept for the meaning of life. The four elements of *ikigai* are (1) what you love, (2) what you're good at, (3) what the world needs, and (4) what you are valued for. An activity walks you through a process to help you determine what *ikigai* means for your WHY and why you can bring a positive outlook for your future.

Chapter 7: WHY Have Empathy for You?

In this chapter, there are stories around stress and how mindfulness strategies can help you breathe and relax, even if life is difficult for you. We are living in an uncertain world that impacts how we handle what we do and how we react to stress. We will discuss the fear of failure, stress vs. burnout, vulnerability, and empathy. Starting with empathy, you can use the design thinking process to identify an issue that is impacting you now and create strategies to help you address that issue.

Chapter 8: WHY Discover your Passions and What you Love?

This chapter walks you through a process to focus on what you love, what makes your heart sing, and why it is helpful to be curious and embrace creativity and Flow. You will discover what drives wonder and why you need an attitude of gratitude. We will share stories about choosing joy and prioritizing your passions to balance your life.

Chapter 9: WHY Align your Passions to What the World Needs?

In this chapter, there are several stories about projects that will make global competence and collaboration real. You will discover the power of connections and moving from ME to WE as you explore the UN Sustainable Development Goals (SDGs). You can dig deeper by exploring how one or more of the targets with one of the SDGs can align with your beliefs to make a positive change globally and locally.

Chapter 10: WHY Your Passion can be Your Message and Grow into your WHY?

In this chapter, you may find that there is one thing you didn't even think was your passion that you can then develop to be your purpose and message. There are several stories about hopes and dreams, sharing what you love, spreading your message, and balancing your life. This chapter will guide you to write your OneWord for the year, your Personal Bill of Rights, and your Elevator Speech.

Chapter 11: WHY Surround Yourself with People who Believe in You?

In this chapter, you can build your Personal Learning Network (PLN) and learn how your believers can support your message. You can share ways to develop your network with people by using questions to ask yourself who believes in you and your message. There are face-to-face opportunities and strategies on how to use social media. Several people share stories about how they built their network along with resources to help you build and grow your own PLN.

Chapter 12: WHY Be the Chief Storyteller of You and Your WHY?

In this chapter, you will learn why you are the best person to share your story and your WHY. Several people will share examples of writing and speaking about being positive, kind, and joyful as they spread their messages. There will be ideas on why your voice matters and how to be your own best advocate. We will discuss why change is difficult and how going out of your comfort zone is the only way for change to happen. When you know your WHY and live it, it is important for you to tell your story before someone else does.

Your WHY and Your Call to Action

No matter who you are or what you do, you can define your WHY by getting to know all about you, your beliefs, strengths, skills, interests, and aspirations. You just need to believe that you are worth caring about and fighting for. When you are passionate about working toward your purpose and own your story about your WHY, then nothing can stop you.

ACKNOWLEDGMENTS

I could not write this book alone. It would not be possible without the support of my family, friends, and colleagues. My family has always been there for me, including my extended family. I dedicated this book to my husband, Tom, who knows me and my WHY better than anyone. I really appreciate my creative children, Sara Zimmerman and Andrew Bray, who have been my best teachers and were very patient as I kept changing careers while searching for my WHY. I'm so fortunate to have three brilliant sisters, Sandy Ritz, Terry Leach, and Janet Ritz. We are eyewitnesses to our history and encourage each other to be the best we can be. My granddaughter, Cali, is very special to me. I love our FaceTime talks, pillow fights, travels together, and was excited to get her approval for my book cover. I miss my mom, who passed over 10 years ago and always read or reviewed whatever I was working on even though she was busy herself. I treasure my time with my amazing mother-in-law, Karen Bray, a quilter and author, who helped me realize how family can be there for each other and why family matters.

I am honored and grateful for the following inspirational thought leaders for their stories and friendship: Nicole Biscotti, Dr. Jim Rickabaugh, Rachelle Dene Poth, Dan Jackson, Lois Letchford, Andelee Espinosa, Michael Mohammad, Shelly Vohra, Mandy Froehlich, Paul Emerich France, Dr. Winston Sakurai, Dr. Lindsay Portnoy, Dr. Jackie Gerstein, Adam Welcome, Dr. Ilene Winokur, Steve Sostak, Darren Ellwein, JoAnn Jacobs, Sylvia Duckworth, Hans Appel, Barbara Gruener, Dave Truss, Jennifer Casa-Todd, Ken Shelton, Tamara Letter, and George Foreman.

I am fortunate to have wonderful friends in and outside of education who have been there along my journey: Dr. Cynthia Chandler, Julie Duffield, Jan Pearson, Nancy Bordenave, Melissa Alden, Rose Colby, Pat Fuschetti, Mary Watrous, Sylvia Crilly, Linda Ullah, Charlotte McGovern, Barbara and George Butko, and Roz Worrall. I'd also like to thank my meetup friends, who help me balance my work life with fun. I am grateful for my journey with Kathleen McClaskey to personalize learning.

I value Dr. Sarah Thomas and appreciate the support I receive from the EduMatch Community for believing in my vision for this book. I am fortunate that Judy Arzt was my editor, who made the best suggestions I needed to clarify the ideas I was trying to get across to my readers. I am grateful for Mandy Froehlich and the process of preparing my book for editing, launching, and marketing.

My professional learning network (PLN) is available all hours of the day and night, challenging my thinking and connecting me to educators around the world. My Twitter #PLN keeps me informed of the latest events and ideas. You can connect to me at @bbray27 and add the hashtags #rethink_learning, #EduMatch, and #defineyourWHY.

1

WHY SHARE YOUR BACKSTORY?

> I am what time, circumstance, history, have made of me, certainly, but I am also, much more than that. So are we all."
>
> — JAMES BALDWIN

Many things happen to us throughout the lives that make us who we are today. Which ones of those experiences impacted you and your decisions? You may not even realize the forces that affected you in your past and may still affect you today.

My Backstory

If you know me, you may not believe that I was actually very shy. If you don't know me, I want to share how my backstory impacted who I am today. As a baby boomer, I have had many experiences and memories. I was brought up to be curious about everything and encouraged to ask questions. My mom always had blank paper with no lines for me to draw whatever I wanted. She made all of my clothes and finger curled my hair to make me look like Shirley Temple. She told me I was beautiful, smart, and could do anything.

| **Figure 1.1 Me as a little girl**

When I went to school, reality hit me. I had trouble fitting in with everyone else. Some of the other kids made fun of my home-made clothes, my curly red hair, and even my being left-handed. I guess I didn't look like everyone else. Actually, the real problem at school was my behavior. I kept asking WHY until finally, I realized that no one was going to answer me. After many WHYs and no answers, I went along to get along and kept my mouth shut.

My life at home was so different than my experiences at school. I had a voice at the dinner table about real questions on real issues. Yet, in school, the teachers did all the talking. We had to learn from textbooks about things that didn't seem relevant. We did stupid worksheets that were just mindless busywork. The school wanted to change me to be right-handed, and my parents fought them. Guess it was because of the desks being made for a right-handed world at that time. We sat in assigned seats in desks bolted to the floor. I was assigned a seat in front of the one boy who decided to make me a target and bully me all year. I had to sit still, fold my hands, keep quiet, and put up with that boy behind me.

I felt like a prisoner in school. I had very few interactions with others and felt invisible, especially when I would complain about the spitballs thrown at my hair. I have tried to forget the names that kids would call me. My hair would frizz up when it rained, and kids would make fun of me. I grew up in Maryland outside of Washington D.C.

and remember the civil rights marches, the riots, and how people of color were treated unfairly. I was feeling sorry for myself but didn't get how my life as a white person was really privileged. Yet, at school, I felt alone and scared and only believed that the way I was treated just didn't seem fair.

Moments in My Life

Before I continue on about what it was like in school, let me go back to tell you about me. I am the oldest of four daughters and am fortunate to have wonderful sisters, Sandy, Terry, and Janet. My first four years of life were in a small apartment in DC, far away from my mom and dad's families in Wisconsin. When I was two, there was an outbreak of polio in our apartment. Several children ended up in iron lungs, and one almost died. I had a lighter case of polio where I couldn't walk or even crawl. I ended up slightly paralyzed for several weeks. Actually, I didn't find out that I had polio until later in life. My parents didn't tell me earlier because they didn't want me to use my sickness as a way for people to feel sorry for me. When I found out when I was older, I asked several of my aunts if that was true, and they said it was. I have one leg shorter than the other, and I'm the shortest person of everyone on both sides of our families. I didn't become a victim, just short with a slight limp.

My dad worked for the government, and because my mom's sister attended communist meetings, he was one of many others called before the McCarthy hearings. The trials were awful for the country and our family, and, through it all, he was suspended and eventually reinstated in his job. Like so many others falsely accused by McCarthy during that time, it impeded the ability to progress in the government, so he left to work in private industry. My mother was a fine artist, a portrait artist, and became a courtroom artist during the trials. As I mentioned earlier, we had deep discussions about life and issues at the dinner table. Yet, all through the trials, my sisters and I never knew what my dad was going through and why my mother was never home. We didn't know that my dad was accused by McCarthy and almost lost his job. We found out later from other family members and through papers we found after our parents passed.

That was in the 50s and 60s when most women stayed home with their children, except my mom. My parents kept things from us so we wouldn't worry. We worried anyway because we knew something was going on, yet, we didn't know what was really happening. My father was going from job to job. He left every morning in a suit. We never knew where he went. Work? Looking for work? At one point, he was gone for months, and we didn't know why. We found out later that he was sent to South Korea and also was an atomic veteran in the Bikini Islands. There were many secrets that we didn't know about my parents, and we're still finding out today. That's another book.

We moved multiple times and went to different neighborhood schools. Many of the women in each neighborhood we lived in were cruel to mom since she was working and, in their words, abandoning her children. I didn't know what she was going through until later. Even though dad was going through a lot, he always used humor and kindness to get us through the day. We never knew he was having problems. In fact, we belonged to a country club where dad played golf every weekend. Mom decided she wanted to be with him and learned how to play golf. She ended up becoming a scratch golfer beating everyone. We never knew how close we were to losing everything and why mom was doing more outside of the home and why my sisters and I were expected to do more in the home.

Those were interesting times with air raid drills, a bomb shelter in our basement, and the civil rights movement. I went to President Kennedy's inauguration and his funeral. I was at almost every parade, especially for events during that time that impacted people's lives. I even went to Martin Luther King's "I Have a Dream" speech. I was way back near the Washington Monument and didn't realize how important that moment was. I was fortunate to be there and wish I could go back and relive it.

Pause/Think/Reflect

Do you have a moment in your life you wish you could go back and relive?

Good Student, Okay Learner

Let me go back to what it was like for me in school. My first-grade teacher labeled kids good or bad. I was always curious and kept asking questions. She didn't allow questions in her class. Because I kept asking questions, I was labeled a troublemaker. I was also labeled as a poor reader. I didn't understand why, because I started reading before I was four. I read words in the paper with my parents. I loved reading to my sisters in a different way. I would take a picture book and use my imagination to create my own stories. My parents knew I loved to read and fought for me. They questioned the teacher, but they were told that I just needed to do the work. I tried to like school. I learned that the best way to make it in her class was to be "good" and do what she told us to do. Even though I was compliant, I was put on a low track in second grade. I had to read books that were too basic for me. I remember a few times faking that I was sick because I was bullied about my hair and clothes. I became the shy, quiet girl in the back of the class. I felt like I didn't belong there.

In third grade, I had a new teacher, Mr. Davis, who believed in the importance of play for learning, being creative, and encouraging everyone's voice. We did group projects. I remember creating a paper-mâché map, sitting wherever we wanted, dancing, and acting in plays. We did a lot of giggling and had fun in class. He took the time to get to know all of us. It was the first time I really enjoyed school and felt like a teacher cared about me.

Halfway through the school year, the classroom changed. The principal was spending time in the back of the room. It looked like Mr. Davis was in trouble and wasn't happy. It wasn't long before learning was back to the same old ways: worksheets and rules that didn't make sense. I missed what we had before. The fourth grade was even stricter, and I only spoke when I was called on. My parents were told that I wasn't going to go very far if I didn't do what I was told. My parents were my advocates, but there weren't that many options for me in the school other than to follow rules.

Nothing much changed in my K-12 world, but I do believe the schools I went to were very good schools for that time. It's just that that was how schools were then. My first-grade teacher labeled me, and I was stuck in a track I couldn't get out. I was bored and sad. A few teachers took the time to get to know me, but most of the time, I just went through the motions and talked to no one. I figured the best thing for me was to learn how to "do" school. I loved learning, but not what I was learning. I was compliant because that's what the system wanted me to be.

I look back and wonder, was it the system or was it me? I didn't know what to believe. I became compliant and did what I was told. I learned how to become a good test taker and how to play the game of "school." I was told by a high school counselor that I should consider a trade instead of college. I didn't believe her. I applied and was accepted to the University of Maryland. Then my father got a job in Northern California. Financially staying in Maryland was not an option. Dad left in January of my senior year. We stayed until I finished school and moved the day after my high school graduation.

That summer in California was the loneliest summer I can remember. I missed out on my graduation parties and left all my friends. I couldn't get into a four-year college in California because it was too late. I ended up going to the local community college, Diablo Valley College (DVC).

Learning and Finding My Voice

DVC was probably one of the best things that happened to me. That's where I found my voice. I took a variety of classes, trying a little of everything. I did well there and realized with the support I received that I could do anything if I put my mind to it. I ended up with a 4.0

GPA. My teachers praised me. I loved writing and wrote a poem that my English teacher said was really good. He asked me to read it to other students at noon. I did, and they loved it. He then published my poem in the school newspaper, and it received wonderful reviews. I started writing more and wrote a short story that I entered into a contest and won. I wrote an article for *Seventeen* magazine and published a book of poems. I loved writing but was not sure how to make a living out of it.

I also loved to dance and started a dance team at DVC with several of my friends with the support of a wonderful teacher, Mrs. Sutton. We were called the Viquettes (the mascot was a Viking). There were 16 of us. I had taken years of dance and choreography. I jumped at the chance to choreograph several of the routines for half times at all the games with my good friend, Roz Worrall, the tall blonde in the middle. We're still good friends today. I'm the short one and the last one on the right.

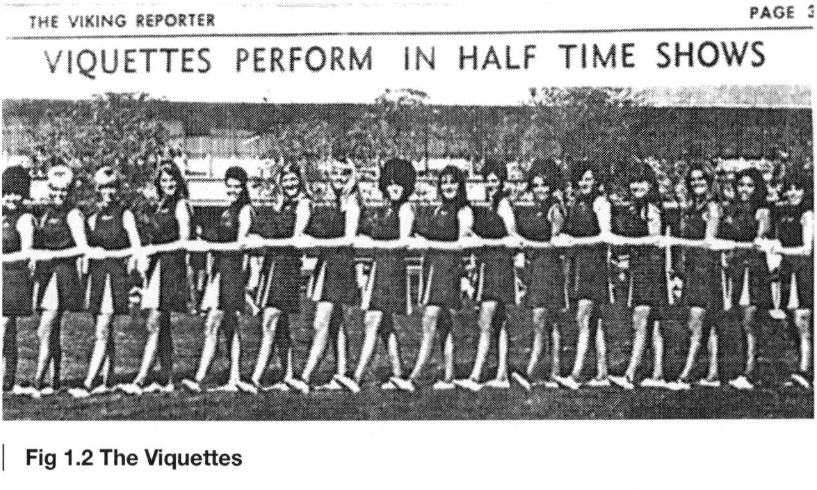
THE VIKING REPORTER PAGE 3

VIQUETTES PERFORM IN HALF TIME SHOWS

Fig 1.2 The Viquettes

I started thinking I could be a dancer, a dance teacher, or a writer. I just didn't believe that I could make a living writing or dancing even though they were my passions. I needed to figure out what I was going to do with my life. It was at that time when a counselor advised me that there was a new Dental Hygiene program starting at DVC. She said my love for science was apparent. I did like my biology and chemistry classes, but I wasn't sure that was what I wanted to do. She encouraged me to apply, so I did. Seven hundred people applied for 18 spots, and I was accepted for one of the spots and became a dental hygienist. I applied because my counselor told me it was a great fit. Was it? I became a hygienist because I got in. I didn't find out until years later that it wasn't my story.

While in school, I fell in love. I met Tom Bray through my sister, Sandy. She was dating him through a high school computer dating program that matched them. Yes, there were computer dating programs then. I remember Sandy coming in and saying she just didn't have that "feeling" for Tom even though he was a great guy. As soon as I met Tom, I had that feeling. I knew. Thanks, Sandy! Tom and I were in love right from the beginning. My parents tried to break us up because we were young with different backgrounds. They kept saying that we were too different and will never make it. They sent me back to live with my Aunt Cele in Pittsburgh, PA during the summer before I started the Dental Hygiene program. I used to spend time with Aunt Cele and enjoyed it. But this time, I cried the whole time I was there. My aunt set me up on dates with different boys who were nice, but they were not Tom. My aunt saw my heartache and said to my mom that it was a mistake to keep us apart from each other. I flew home after a few months. We were married as soon as I finished the hygiene program. We were young and in love. We're still married 49 years later. Love wins!

| Fig 1.3 Married

Dental Flossing to Mental Flossing

I got a job right out of school working for a wonderful dentist, Dr. McGovern, five days a week. It was a good job with a great staff. I made a great salary with benefits while Tom was finishing school. After two years of working there, something happened. One day, Dr. McGovern was acting strange and was saying goodbye to everyone in an odd way. I didn't realize that would be the last time I would see him. He decided to end his life that night. It was devastating for his family and for all of us. I felt guilty because I should have known. I had that strange feeling something was wrong. Now I remember that feeling when someone talks to me about their life and giving up.

I continued working for different dentists even when I became a mom of two beautiful, amazing children, Sara and Andrew. I had told myself I wouldn't work when my children were little because my mom had to work, but we needed both of our incomes. I loved every minute of being a mom. If I could change one thing, I would have taken more time off with my children when they were young. I really missed special moments when they were little and can never bring those moments back.

I was asked to teach dental hygiene at the local college and enrolled in San Francisco State University's education program. I continued as a hygienist and taught for four years. Then when my children were in school, I got involved in the PTA and volunteered in the school on my days off. It was during that time when I noticed how cool computers were. I mean, I had to have the first computer that came out, take it apart, and put it back together again. I needed to know how they worked. It was also then that the school needed someone to help with computers. I took classes, got my credentials to teach computer and gifted classes. I even redesigned an extra room, actually a large closet, into a computer lab over several weekends with the principal. We even added another doorway. I was pretty proud of that room and the program I helped create.

I had to have one of the first personal computers that came out and wanted to learn every software program available, video production, coding, and more. I went through a Master's program in educational technology and leadership. I still did dental hygiene a few days a week, but the rest of the time, I found every opportunity to teach. I was a Chapter Leader for the Young Astronauts, a Girl Scout leader, a Den Mother, and taught Gifted and Talented classes. I taught computer classes for all grade levels, including adult learning classes. I also taught clear credential courses for pre-service teachers at several local universities. I loved every moment of teaching.

In 1987, something happened that changed everything for me. We were having our house remodeled, and the contractor was finishing the deck, but there was no way to keep my dog off the deck. I went to get her off the deck and ended up tripping, falling off or through the deck and hitting my leg and my head. I was unconscious for some time stuck underneath the deck. I remember the fireman couldn't get me out from under the deck because I was squeezed in too tight. My daughter, Sara, who was 10 at that time, got a leaf from the table to give to the firemen, and it worked. The firemen told me how clever she was. Yes, she is.

I broke my right ankle with my leg pretty messed up and was in a full cast for 4 months. During the time I was healing, I didn't realize how bad my neck was until after the cast was off. I had to have three of my vertebrae in my neck fused because my fingers and one foot were going numb. I look back and realize how lucky I was. I could have died.

Even though I was badly hurt, it was the beginning of exciting times for me. I was a dental hygienist for 20 years, and, for me, it was a job. When I started teaching dental hygiene, something changed for me. I was excited about teaching. I started working in my kids' preschool and elementary school. I wanted to learn more about empowering students, so I took classes about education and technology while I continued working part-time as a hygienist. I found every opportunity I could to teach. I wish I had known what I loved earlier. My sister, Sandy, coined the phrase for me: "Dental Flossing to Mental Flossing."

> Looking back, I just wonder who I would be now if I knew
> I wanted to teach and write and had found my voice earlier.

Searching for My Why and Purpose

I've always loved reading even if I was told I was a poor reader. I think now it was because I had trouble focusing. Even though I was labeled, no one had tested me for dyslexia or ADHD. I had some challenges but figured out a way to get through school. I do know that I really enjoyed hearing stories about others. I was also interested in connecting people and learning about their stories. When I started teaching teachers how to use technology, that was my WHAT and their HOW.

In the early 90s, I started an online community in YahooGroups called TechStaffDevelop for teachers and leaders that focused on technology professional development. There were over 400 educators from all over the world. YahooGroups was the first social network that seemed to work at that time. What's interesting is that I'm still connected to many of the people I met way back then.

In 2000, I created an online platform, My eCoach (https://my-ecoach.com), for educators to have a place where they could tell their stories, post lessons, and connect with other educators. The reason I built this was that Oakland USD teachers were asked to create class websites and post daily. It was my job to train them to create their websites and FTP every night. That was just too difficult for them. We needed an easier way for them to connect, collaborate, and post lessons. With the help of an amazing team, we created an online coaching site where teachers could get virtual help from a coach or another teacher.

My motto for My eCoach that I trademarked in 2002 was *"Making Learning Personal."* My eCoach took TechStaffDevelop beyond email and allowed collaboration, connecting, building teams, blogs, websites, surveys, quizzes, citations, standards alignment tools, and more for sharing together. The eLibrary now has over 50,000 resources that members shared for others to use. I was fortunate to meet many people from around the world through this platform, and almost 21,000 people are using it today.

I started connecting on social media on Twitter in 2007 before it was big, and was amazed at what I could learn in 140 characters from people in my personal learning network (PLN). My handle is

@bbray27. I love that Twitter now allows for 280 characters in a tweet, plus you can add images, links, videos, and tag people to grow your #PLN (Personal Learning Network). I'm able to connect to people, curate resources, collaborate, and more on Twitter and other social media platforms along with My eCoach.

I always believed I was supposed to share stories and to help others tell their stories. I started my blog, Rethinking Learning, in 2004 in My eCoach. After five years and hundreds of blog posts later, I decided in 2009 to move my blog to my WordPress site. My daughter, Sara, and her husband, Rob Zimmerman, created my website, Rethinking Learning. Sara created a brand, designed my logo, and personalized my site for me, along with other marketing materials. https://barbarabray.net

I took the WHAT to a new level.

| Fig. 1.4 Rethinking Learning Banner

I invited educators, authors, and change agents to share their stories on my site. I took a detour in 2012 when Kathleen McClaskey and I started Personalize Learning, LLC, because there was confusion around the terms personalization, differentiation, and individualization (PDI). We created the PDI chart and a course around the 5 W's (What, Who, Where, Wow, and Why). From 2012 to 2017, we worked with schools around the nation and co-authored two books: *Make Learning Personal* (Bray, B. & McClaskey, 2015) and *How to Personalize Learning* (Bray, B. & McClaskey, 2017). Thousands of schools and districts around the U.S. and other countries have used our charts and books to guide the design of learner-centered environments. We are both proud of what we did to define and implement personalized learning.

After writing the books, I believed something was missing for me. My WHY. I wanted to write and share stories but in a different direction than what we were doing. In fact, both of us were starting to spread our wings. We decided to go our separate ways and closed our business in 2017 to do what we do best. I began focusing on the WHY instead of our work that started with the WHAT. I realized I needed to update the charts and resources to reflect this change. My new resources are in my toolkit: https://barbarabray.net/toolkit/

I realized that my WHY at that time were the connections I had made. I wanted to learn about their stories. I started my Rethinking Learning podcast in 2017 as a new beginning for me. Actually, it was challenging for me to learn how to set up a podcast that really captured the person I was having a conversation with. I was curious about them and their lives. I knew there was a more creative way to create the podcast and expand it with a complementary blog post. I was lucky that my son, Andrew, was a sound designer and willing to help me experiment and try different platforms and tools. In fact, my first podcast was a practice session with Andrew, and it turned out pretty good, so we published his conversation as Episode #1. https://barbarabray.net/podcasts/

A few months later, I started the #rethink_learning Twitter chat with my co-host Shelly Vohra @raspberryberet3, that we do every other Monday evening. We invite guest hosts to lead the conversations around emerging topics. These past few years have been an exciting time for me to learn and grow. I have been writing more posts, invited to write articles, and asked to provide testimonials and excerpts for my author friends. I'm watching TedTalks, participating in the TED Masterclass with ISTE, and am learning how to become a better speaker. I am building out my platform, My eCoach, to encourage people to connect, collaborate, share their stories, build websites, create online courses, and blog. One thing I know is that the older you get, the more you realize that you can learn from mistakes. I know because I've made way too many. You just have to forgive yourself and keep trying new things.

 You don't learn to walk by following rules. You learn by doing, and by falling over."

— RICHARD BRANSON

Activity: Build Your Backstory

All of us have a backstory. Our lives are much more than this moment. What is your backstory? Start a journal using a paper or digital version, whichever works best for you. On the first page, title it **My Story to Discover My Purpose.** Date it. You can write anything on this page, draw, write your dreams, or keep it blank. On the next page, title it **My Backstory** and start writing about your backstory by answering any of the following questions or come up with your own questions:

- What events stand out that impacted who you are today?
- What was it like when you were young?
- Where did you grow up?
- What was your family of origin like for you?
- Did you have siblings, and what was your order in your family?
- If you are an only child, what was your experience growing up?
- What was school like when you were young?
- When did you notice a change in you? What happened?

You can keep some pages blank if you want to add more to this section.

Activity: Build Your Event Chart

In everyone's life, some events stand out and others impact you, some in good ways and some in not very good ways. An Event Chart doesn't have to be a timeline. It's about the events that stand out in your life as opportunities and obstacles.

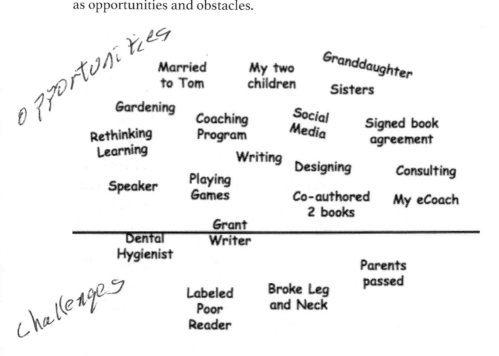

| Fig. 1.5 Event Chart

I created my Event Chart in Google Drawing about events and people that stand out in my life. I brainstormed who means the most to me. My family always comes first. I'm fortunate to have a wonderful husband, Tom, who believes in me. Two amazing children, Sara and Andrew, who are creative geniuses and love to challenge me. I have three brilliant sisters, Sandy, Terry, and Janet, who are as curious as I am and we have great talks about everything. My granddaughter, Cali, just shines and is the light of my life. I love the time with my family and extended family (nieces, nephews, their children, my mother-in-law, my son-in-law, and all the husbands and wives). I treasure every moment with them. Family is everything.

We live in the Oakland, California hills on ½ an acre with a lot of room to garden. Actually, I love to plan the garden and watch my husband create and maintain it. He keeps all the plants, vegetables, fruit trees, and flowers alive. I love to sit and read in my hammock or even work outside on a clear day. I'm fortunate to have lived in our house in the best neighborhood for almost 45 years. We have potlucks, parties, and watch out for each other. Most everyone has a garden, and many have bees and some have chickens. Yes, I said Oakland. You're probably wondering, "farms in Oakland?" No, not a farm, but it is a great place to live.

I'm kind of hooked on Twitter and other social media. I have met many amazing people online and then connected to them later face-to-face. I am blessed with wonderful friends. Some I have known for years who I treasure. I try to find time to either call them to catch up or meet them if they have time. A group of friends and I play Mahjong weekly, and another group plays poker once a month. We even have a group of us through Meetup.com that set up game days to play board games all night long or several days on a retreat. I love playing games and challenging myself through games.

The line delineates those events that impacted me below as challenges and above as opportunities. You probably notice that Grant Writer straddles the line. I wrote many grants and was awarded several of them. However, there were too many that took months to write and were not awarded. When I was in the middle of writing a grant, my parents were there for me and really influenced me. My dad helped me with my business until he was diagnosed with Alzheimer's. My mom would check in with me often and helped bounce ideas off of me. Then my mother was diagnosed with lung cancer. When they both passed within months of each other after long illnesses, it was tough. I put their passing below the line because of how those times being with them when they were failing affected me. I now know that every moment I had with them was a gift. I really miss them. Our lives take on multiple dimensions. My event chart will probably change because of new adventures, events, and people along my journey.

On the next page in your journal, start your Event Chart. Choose as many events or people as you want that mean something to you. You can add your events to post-it notes or just doodle on your Event Chart in your journal.

Questions to Ponder

1. Is there a time that you would like to go back to and live again? Why?
2. Is there something that you wish you could do over and maybe change?
3. If you could go back and talk to someone from long ago, who would that be? What would you want to talk about?
4. How do you think your backstory impacted you, so you became who you are today?

Wonderings

I look back on my life and wonder about the choices I made. I wonder what my life would be like if I stayed in Maryland and went to school to become a teacher instead of a dental hygienist. What would my life be like now? I would not have met my husband and had our beautiful, amazing children. Even if some things were difficult, I see my life as a journey on different paths. Each path made me who I am today. Have you ever wondered about the choices you made and your journey you went on to become YOU today? This book is for you to explore your path, your journey.

* * *

If you are looking for additional resources and more about this chapter, go to:

- the book study questions, go to https://barbarabray.net
- digital resources, go to http://bit.ly/defineyourwhy-digital
- discussions on Twitter, use the hashtag #defineyourWHY

WHY BE THE MAIN CHARACTER OF YOUR STORY?

 "The whole story is about you. You are the main character."

— DON MIGUEL RUIZ

Your story is about you. Everyone has a story. You are you. You are unique. There is no one like you in the whole world. You know you better than anyone else. Even though you know *you*, you may not know some important things about *you*. Where do you begin?

Choose a Favorite Book or Character

Think of yourself as the main character in a book you may write one day. Even if you don't want to write a book, you can learn from literary characters to help you define *you*. Consider a book you loved and its main character's qualities. I will be asking you to write about several of the qualities (good or bad) that defined that character.

I did this. I was learning how to write and was told that I had to develop my character first for my readers to connect and relate to them. I wasn't sure how to do that. I decided to find a book with a character I liked and wanted to learn more about. One of my favorite books is an autobiography *West with the Wind* by Beryl Markham (Markham, 1983). The first paragraph engaged me to want to read more.

> *How is it possible to bring order out of memory? I should like to begin at the beginning, patiently, like a weaver at his loom. I should like to say, "This is the place to start; there can be no other."*

Beryl Markham's writing was like poetry, and her story was incredible. Ernest Hemingway knew her and described her writing. Here is an excerpt of what he wrote on the back cover of the book.

> *I was completely ashamed of myself as a writer. I felt that I was simply a carpenter with words...she can write rings around all of us."*

> — ERNEST HEMINGWAY

Describe the Main Character

I took out my journal, and as I read each chapter, I started a section called Main Character, Beryl Markham, and added characteristics about her. Here are the four characteristics I thought stood out the most for this amazing woman:

- Adventurous
- Risk-taker
- Determined
- Brave

A little about Beryl Markham first before I describe her characteristics. She was born in England in 1902, and in 1906 grew up in East Africa on her father's farm, where he bred racehorses. This book is her story recounting all of her adventures about lions, narrow escapes, winning horse races, being a pilot who carried mail and passengers to all corners of East Africa (including being abandoned in the desert), and being the first person to fly solo from Paris to New York though crashing in Nova Scotia. She was the perfect character for me to start with. I wanted those same characteristics I identified about her that I wrote in my journal, but those were Beryl's, not mine. My life is different than hers.

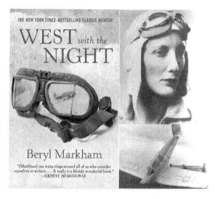

Fig. 2.1 West with the Night by Beryl Markham
(Markham, 1983)

While I was reading and writing down her qualities, I couldn't even imagine a woman doing all the things she did during the 1920s and

30s. She was *adventurous* by pushing herself to try new things. Going across the Atlantic by herself from Paris to the U.S. was more than being *brave*; it meant taking life-threatening *risks*. I can't even imagine a person today doing half of what she accomplished. She had to be *determined* to keep pushing herself. I added comments and questions with the words that described her.

- How was she that brave?
- Was she aware that being the first person flying solo westward across the Atlantic from Paris to the U.S. was historical? Plus, she was a woman flying solo across the Atlantic in 1936 before a man did that.
- How come I never heard of her before I read this book?
- Why did she train and ride racehorses?
- How did she keep persisting and challenging herself throughout her life?

I've read *West with the Wind* many times since I first found her book in the 90s. I love her writing, her story, and her as the main character. I would love to be able to write like her. I am definitely not a risk-taker like her, but I am determined to do what I believe is best for learners of all ages. I do persist and fight for what I believe. That's why I'm writing this book.

Consider What Describes YOU Best

If I decided to define my WHY, I needed to get to know me and reflect on who I was up to that time. I needed to understand me as the main character in my life, my story, and consider the words that best describe me. That was difficult for me to think of *me* as a character in a book that I would like to connect to, but I did come up with four qualities to start with from what people have said about me.

- **Curious.** Yes. That's the first quality I want to wrap my hands around. I've always been curious, asking loads of questions. I remember my mom told my sisters and me to not be afraid to ask questions. In fact, she said that if someone asks you a question, go deeper. Ask a question back. I remember wondering why there were that many stars in the sky or why the clouds looked like animals drifting by. I like being curious. I really feel that's a good quality to start with.

- **Kind.** I found doing random acts of kindness for no reason made me feel really good. After the fires in Oakland in 1991, I was at a coffee shop when I noticed several firemen behind me. I was really grateful for all they do for us and bought them whatever they wanted to drink or eat. Several times, I've paid for the person behind me at a toll booth. I've let others go before me in line at the grocery store. I listen to others who contact me and try to provide an ear when they need it. It feels good to do things for others. I'm not planning what to do. I'm just trying to be aware of those around me and look for ways to listen and be kind. Sometimes, it just happens, and I feel fortunate that I can be there when someone is in need of a hug or for someone to listen. I added caring people in this book who spread kindness as their passions.

- **Silly.** I have a problem when I start laughing. I start giggling, and it turns into a crazy belly laugh. I also like to play, especially with my granddaughter, Cali. We'll have pillow fights, squirt water guns on a hot day, and enjoy going to Disneyland and riding Thunder Mountain loads of times. When I listen to the conversations in my podcast, I hear my giggle. I guess I need to listen and control that more, or not. I guess that's just me. Sometimes, I laugh too hard that I can't even talk. My family has evidence. They've taken videos of me laughing. Here is an embarrassing video that my daughter took of me:

Barbara laughing:
https://youtu.be/tOD5yuxUo1c

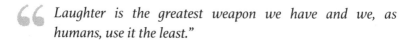

> "*Laughter is the greatest weapon we have and we, as humans, use it the least.*"

— MARK TWAIN

- **Creative.** I cannot draw like my mom, who was an artist, my daughter (who is also an artist, crochets, writes, and plays the drums), or my son, who is an actor, musician, voice coach, sound designer, and musical director. My husband plays the sax, knits, builds things, and gardens. Everyone around me is creative. I love to dance, but later in life, I realized how much I enjoyed writing and designing. I was exposed to the design thinking process and wanted to experiment with it. I enjoy writing curriculum, designing new learning spaces, learning how to code, and developing databases. I love any opportunity to create, design, experiment, and try new things.

Questions Lead to More Questions

I took these four words and put them on post-it notes on the wall in front of me. What did I think about those words? Could I connect to someone who was curious, kind, silly, and creative? What questions do I have for my character? I used post-it notes again to come up with questions. These are the top five that stuck out for me.

- What do I do now to be curious?
- Does my curiosity help me become more creative?
- How do I keep myself focused on being creative and my writing?
- Am I silly more than I am serious?
- How can we encourage kindness in schools?
- What can I do to spread kindness?

Each question led to new questions. Is this a character I want people to read about? Why would my readers like my character? What makes my character interesting, exciting, and someone with a purpose?

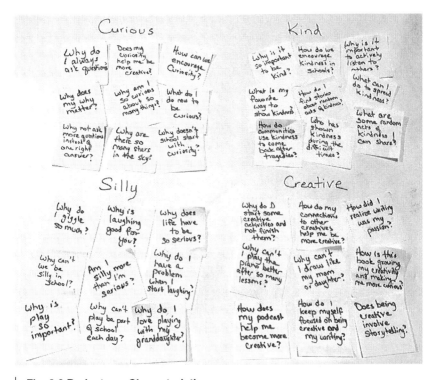

| Fig. 2.2 Brainstorm Characteristics

All of a sudden, when I did this activity, I realized I didn't know my story as well as I thought I did to share it with you. All of these questions kept pouring out of me. I wasn't done. There were more questions, and I wondered if these four characteristics were the right ones to push me forward to make my character unique. That's when it hit me. It was right there in front of me.

I believe I'm a storyteller. Is that my purpose? I need to keep working on it to see if this is what my passion is. How can I make others believe what I think is my purpose if I'm not sure? Back to what I said in the introduction: *our purpose changes with our experiences.* When we learn or master something, maybe it opens the door to develop a new passion, which leads to a different purpose.

 When you are a bear of very little brain, and you think of things, you find sometimes that a Thing which seemed very thingish inside you is quite different when it gets out into the open and has other people looking at it."

— A. A. Milne (Winnie the Pooh)

WHY Write

I met Nicole Biscotti on Twitter and knew I wanted to get to know her better. I had great conversations with her about the book she is writing with her son, Jason, for EduMatch Publishing. I knew her story would resonate with my readers. I remember her telling me she had two books she wanted to write; one about her grandmother and the other with her son. I listened and read her summaries and knew the story with her son was more relevant and urgent. His story made it urgent, especially given he was young and could speak effectively about his experiences and feelings. I looked forward to their book and asked her to write about her WHY in writing it.

* * *

Writing about ADHD with My Son Jason
by Nicole Biscotti, M.Ed.

When I had a son with ADHD, everything changed in my
world, starting with my own perspective. Calls poured in from
the school reporting cleared classrooms because of Jason's
outbursts, administrators chasing him across campus, and
Jason in a restraint. I watched teachers struggle with my son,
some with perseverance and compassion bordering on saintly,
and others with obvious frustration and even anger. I watched
as my son felt the pain of disappointing his teachers and
myself and rejection from peers. I saw his self-esteem sink as
he began to think that he was not "good at school." I watched
all of this happening and felt completely helpless.

Jason is not the only child struggling to be successful in
school while he manages the symptoms of ADHD. How many
children are internalizing that they are "bad" because they are
constantly punished for behaviors that they are not fully able
to control? I promise you the missed recess doesn't scar, it's
believing that their teacher, who they so want to please, is
"mad" at them. Why does is rarely occur to us that school can
be designed differently to help these children realize their
potential? Would we have the ability to make changes to our
classroom and our curriculum if we thought they were in the
best interest of our students? As parents, how can we support
our children?

I am a teacher with advanced degrees and a mother of four.
None of that prepared me for helping Jason. It took me years
to understand how to advocate for and to support my son in
school. This has been a very emotionally expensive professional development that has forever impacted my practice. I
know that there are parents with less knowledge and
resources, feeling helpless while their child struggles. I also

know that teachers have not been adequately supported as we've moved to the Inclusion Model in schools. Many well-intentioned adults care deeply but don't know how to help children with ADHD. As an educator, I care deeply that every child has access to quality education. I began to realize that our journey was an opportunity and that the journaling that we were doing was the beginning of telling our story.

Jason is unique because he is willing to share personal experiences, exceptionally direct, self-aware, and articulate for his age. When I question continuing this project, I think of all of the children failing, being suspended, expelled, and ending up in our prison system and the pain that they've acquired along the way. I think of the anguish and stress that parents and teachers are feeling. I believe that by sharing our story, Jason and I can bridge understanding among children, parents, and teachers. I hope that through increased understanding, we can better meet the needs of the growing population of kids with ADHD. My dream is that they are successful academically and can develop their unique talents in our schools. This is WHY I am writing about growing up with ADHD with my son Jason.

Twitter: @BiscottiNicole
Website: https://nicolebiscotti.wordpress.com
Episode #85: Writing to Uplift, Inform, and Bridge Understanding with Nicole Biscotti
http://bit.ly/episode85-biscotti

 Believe in yourself and all that you are. Know that there is something inside of you that is greater than any obstacle."

— Christian D. Larson

Activity: Discover and Define the Main Character

Let's build your main character for the story of your life. Choose a book that you like as much as I like *West with the Wind*. Start the next section in your journal to define the main character in the book you chose.

- On the first page, title it **My Story to Discover My Purpose.** Date it. You can write anything on this page, draw, write your dreams, or keep it blank.
- Read. I mean read a lot of different books, fiction, and non-fiction.
- Find that one book where the main character resonates with you. Not sure which book to focus on? I added a list of books as resources at the end of this chapter for you.
- Go to the next page in your journal and write down every quality that the main character or a character in the book you like has. Choose four or more to list in your journal.
- Brainstorm questions in your journal about each of the qualities in relation to the character in the book you chose. Write if any of those qualities are why you connected or didn't connect to that character.
- Share any thoughts about this process in your journal.
- What did you learn about this character?
- Did this process help you understand the character better or make you want to reread sections of the book?

Activity: Now, Build YOU as the Main Character

- Start a new page in your journal and title it **Me as the Main Character.**
- Write down as many characteristics about you as you can.
- Choose four and describe why each of those qualities stood out about you.

- Brainstorm questions you would ask about the qualities as they relate to you as the main character.
- Come back and look at the four qualities and descriptions. Do they sound like you? Do the four characteristics with the descriptions make sense? Would someone else want to know more about your character because of the characteristics?
- If they are the right four qualities, then review the questions. Go ahead and add more or change any of the questions. If one or two of the characteristics need to change or be tweaked, go ahead and do that now.

Have some fun with your character

I mentioned this idea of describing the main character to Dr. Lindsay Portnoy @lportnoy, who gave me an idea to push it out on Twitter. She suggested that I ask my PLN (Personal Learning Network) what is the genre of their book and the fictional landscape as the background of their story.

Did you know...

YOU are the main character in your story?

What genre is your book?

What fictional landscape is the backdrop of your story?

Fig. 2.3 Main Character of Your Story

I created a graphic with this question and tweeted it out. There were many responses and even more questions that led to more responses. Just a few here...

Nicole Biscotti, M. Ed. 👏 💜 @BiscottiNicole · Jan 10
Replying to @bbray27 @lportnoy and 8 others
I love this because when we view our lives from this perspective we're willing to see things more objectively and even with humor. 💜

◯   ⟲ 2   💜 10   ⬆

Dr. Monica Housen @MonicaHousen · Jan 10
Replying to @bbray27 @lportnoy and 8 others
I like these Qs b/c they remind me that my story is MINE, and I am free to change it. I wonder how much I can really change though, and still be ME. My genre is probably something like travel-adventure. The landscape? Scenic, with a good dose of sarcasm and irony.

◯   ⟲ 4   💜 11   ⬆

Kate Lindquist @heARTISTatWORK · Jan 11
Replying to @bbray27 @lportnoy and 7 others
I love questions like this. Makes me reflect...I'm gonna say that mine is a mashup of each genre...as each chapter in my life, heck each out of my day, is a beautiful conglomeration of fantasy, fiction, horror, mystery, comedy, etc. all in the wonderful world of Kateness!

◯   ⟲   ♡ 4   ⬆

Fig. 2.4 Twitter Feed

As you go on your journey to discover you, you can connect with others as I did. Social media helps me connect with like-minded people and some who don't think like me who stretch my thinking. I know some teachers and librarians who love encouraging discussions or using technology like this with their students to build a community around their main characters in books. Think about Chapter 2 on the main characters as an activity to support you and as an introduction to developing your WHY.

List of Books by Author and Main Characters

- *The Great Gatsby* by F. Scott Fitzgerald (Jay Gatsby)
- *The Catcher in the Rye* by J.D.Salinger (Holden Caulfield)
- *Becoming* by Michelle Obama (autobiography)
- *Breakfast at Tiffany's* by Truman Capote (Holly Golightly)
- *Alice's Adventures in Wonderland* by Lewis Carroll (The Mad Hatter)
- *Matilda* by Roald Dahl (Matilda)
- *The Chronicles of Narnia* by C.S. Lewis (Aslan)
- *The Book Thief* by Markus Zusak (Liesel Meminger)
- *The Hobbit* by J.R.R. Tolkien (Gandalf)
- *West with the Wind* by Beryl Markham (autobiography)

Go ahead and share more books to the list on this Google Doc:

http://bit.ly/maincharacter-WHY

Questions to Ponder

- What did you learn that was new about *you* or never thought was *you*?
- What did you find interesting about *you* as the main character?
- What was missing about *you* as the main character?

- Do you see a glimmer of the purpose behind all the words and characteristics?

Wonderings

This is the beginning of a new you. You are complex. There is more about you that others may not know. You have your own story, and it is amazing. People will wonder why they didn't know this or that about you. When you share your purpose and your story, you will be amazed by the reactions people share with you. I don't know how you feel now, but I'm excited to learn about you and follow your journey. Be the best YOU today!

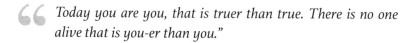 *Today you are you, that is truer than true. There is no one alive that is you-er than you."*

— Dr. Seuss

* * *

If you are looking for additional resources and more about this chapter, go to:

- the book study questions, go to https://barbarabray.net
- digital resources, go to http://bit.ly/defineyourwhy-digital
- discussions on Twitter, use the hashtag #defineyourWHY

WHY START WITH YOUR WHY?

> *Don't quit. Never give up trying to build the world you can see, even if others can't see it. Listen to your drum and your drum only. It's the one that makes the sweetest sound."*

— SIMON SINEK

I have been following Simon Sinek's work for a long time. He says in his book, *Start with Why* (2009), that people are inspired by a sense of purpose. He also believes that Why should come first when communicating before the "How" and "What." Sinek calls this the Golden Circle, which is like a target with the "Why" as the bullseye in the inner circle. Sinek's book has opened my eyes to the WHY and ideas for my business.

The Golden Circle

Sinek explains that many of us start with the what or, in some cases, the how. But without the why, we are not as motivated to do what we do. Most of Sinek's work is to support marketing, an organization's WHY, and what a business or organization is promoting. I found that educators and others who I coached needed to know their WHY, then their WHAT, before the HOW. I adapted Sinek's Golden Circle to represent what it means to define your WHY for your personal growth.

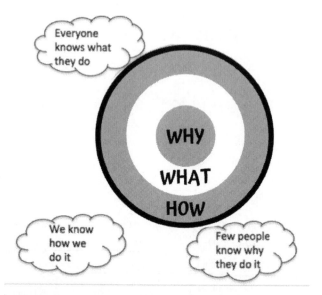

Fig. 3.1 Simon Sinek's Golden Circle Changed from WHY to WHAT then HOW

Let me take the Golden Circle deeper.

Why = The Purpose
This is about what you believe.

What = The Goal
The desired result to reach your purpose.

How = The Process
The specific actions you take to realize your WHY.

Sinek works with leadership teams and helps organizations find the WHY. He has another book called *Find Your Why* (Sinek, 2017). In reading both of his books and watching his videos, I felt that the Golden Circle and his strategies in starting with the WHY as something anyone could use. I believe that it is not just about finding your purpose for your business, team, organization, or what you do for your work. It can also be about finding your WHY for you.

Activity: Reflect on Knowing your WHY

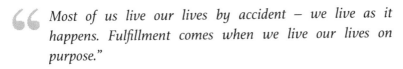

> *Most of us live our lives by accident – we live as it happens. Fulfillment comes when we live our lives on purpose."*

— SIMON SINEK

When I read Simon Sinek's quote above, it reminded me of Michael Jr.'s video "Know Your Why."

| https://youtu.be/LZe5y2D60YU

Before you read the rest of this chapter, please watch the video referenced above. Michael Jr. asked an audience member, who was a music teacher, to sing two versions of a song. I'd like you to reflect on the video in your journal.

- How did it make you feel when you heard his first version of his song?

- How did it make you feel when you listened to the second version?
- How does this video reflect Simon Sinek's quote about "living our lives by accident or living our lives on purpose?

Clarity of Purpose

I was fortunate to have a conversation on my podcast with Dr. Jim Rickabaugh, who was the Director, and now is the Senior Advisor of the Institute of Personalized Learning. We talked about the WHY and his new work, *Starting with WHY*. I agree with his perspective that when you know the WHY, then you need a compelling WHAT that relates to your WHY before moving to the HOW. Jim shared his ideas of the WHY that made sense. I asked him if he would share his story about the WHY and why it is important for personal development and learning.

* * *

Defining the Vision, Clarifying the Work, Offering Freedom in the Approach
Dr. Jim Rickabaugh @drrickabaugh

Purpose is among the most powerful motivators of behavior known to humankind. A compelling sense of purpose can drive people to take on challenges they never imagined and persist when victory is far from certain. Clarity of purpose gives meaning and purpose to our lives, our work, and our relationships. It answers for us the question: WHY?

When joined by WHAT and HOW, purpose moves to focus and action. Daniel Pink, in his book, *Drive: The Surprising Truth About What Motivates Us*, describes the combination of WHY, WHAT, and HOW in the powerful motivators he identifies as purpose (WHY), mastery (WHAT), and autonomy

(HOW). He notes that when all three are present high levels of motivation are near certain.

However, these three concepts also relate to each other. There is a sequence that taps the powerful synergy these three elements offer. We have discovered that purpose, or WHY, is the main driver. It defines what is important and frames the focus of attention and energy. Without a clear and compelling WHY, WHAT, and HOW can lose much of their leverage.

For us, WHY speaks to our commitment to nurturing powerful, flexible, and independent learners who can be successful in a rapidly changing future rather than being satisfied with proficient students who can perform well in a controlled and predictable classroom.

The magic of a clear and compelling WHY is revealed in how it helps to define WHAT work needs to be done. It points to the knowledge, skills, and dispositions learners will need to be successful. For example, knowing how to learn will be more useful and important than being skilled at being taught. Taking ownership of learning will be key to moving forward when no formal teacher is present.

The magic of this sequence of WHY, WHAT, and HOW is revealed in the flexibility, autonomy, and creativity that can be a part of the strategies, approaches, and creativity tapped to address WHAT is important while remaining aligned with WHY the work matters so much.

When we began the work at the Institute for Personalized Learning, we spent many hours and endured seemingly endless conversations about WHY redesigning the experience of learners was so important and WHY it mattered. We challenged our shared experience as educators in which WHAT and HOW had dominated our thinking, too often ignoring the importance of WHY, and assuming there must be a good reason for ways things had been done in the past.

Ultimately, we came to understand that clarity about our compelling shared purpose, or our WHY, would make the investment worth making and the risks worth taking. Our WHY told us WHAT needed to be done. The combination of these two elements freed educators to bring their best, creative selves to work each day, week, and year. It provided freedom for educators to be flexible in HOW they would engage students in learning, as long as it was aligned with the WHAT and WHY of the work.

Over the past decade, we have watched the power of WHY, WHAT, and HOW to create meaning, purpose, clarity, and flexibility in the professional lives of educators. It has restored the passion, commitment, and satisfaction that so many educators have missed for far too long.

Senior Advisor at the Institute of Personalized Learning: http:// www.cesa1.k12.wi.us/

Jim's Books:
Frontier, T. and Rickabaugh, J. (2014) Five Levers to Improve Learning: How to Prioritize for Powerful Results in Your School. Alexandria, VA: ASCD.

Rickabaugh, J. (2016) Tapping the Power of Personalized Learning: A roadmap for school leaders. Alexandria, VA: ASCD.
Episode #60 Podcast/Post: Start with Why and Stay with Why with Dr. Jim Rickabaugh
http://bit.ly/episode60-rickabaugh

Searching for Your WHY While Doing Your WHAT

Let's consider pre-service teachers who are taught WHAT to teach and the theories behind the WHAT they are asked to do. It tends to be all about the content based on the single-subject or multi-subject credential they are working on. After you began teaching, you probably started with the WHAT and never knew WHY you were teaching that way. If you were like me, on the first day of school, you shared the class rules and classroom expectations and never questioned them. I did the same for my sixth-graders and when I taught dental hygiene. I never provided opportunities for my students to ask WHY they were doing things the way they were doing them or WHY dental hygiene is a notable profession.

I was doing professional development at Oakland Unified School District as part of the Core Values Grades fourth-eighth project for five years, and then Urban Dreams 9th-12th grades another four years. During the projects, there were way too many questions about the WHAT around classroom behavior and discipline. Actually, I still get questions from teachers about those issues. When you start with the WHAT as the teacher, you usually are the one held responsible and accountable for the learning. Too many teachers have told me that there is no room for the WHY. They have told me over and over again that they do not have the time to get to know the kids in their class(es), especially secondary teachers who may have 150 or more students in six or seven periods. I've known some middle and high school teachers who told me they teach multiple subjects and are responsible for extra-curricular activities. I've heard, *"TIME for planning or TIME for me. What's that?"* In these cases, teachers continue to do what they have always done to cover the curriculum because that is what they are mandated to do and have time for.

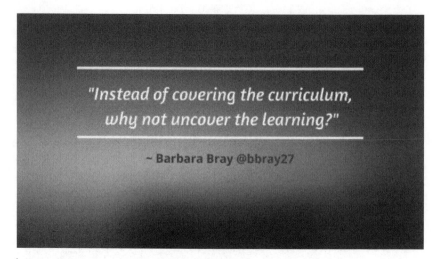

"Instead of covering the curriculum,
why not uncover the learning?"

~ Barbara Bray @bbray27

| Fig. 3.2. Bray Quote uncover the learning

When I started my consulting business in the early 90s, I was an educational technology specialist teaching teachers HOW to integrate technology. I never asked them if they knew their WHY about using technology. I assumed they wanted to learn the HOW. Remember, technology was pretty new in the classroom then, and most had only one to four computers to share with the whole class. After looking back at that time, I remember creating step-by-step guides so they could refer to them when they didn't know HOW to do something. I had over 200 guides that I shared in the workshops and in online classes. I didn't make them all. I had a team of amazing designers and coaches. When I visited the classrooms after they participated in the workshops to witness their progress, my eyes were opened. Too many teachers were hesitant or resistant to using computers. They were not even considering integrating them into the curriculum. One teacher had black plastic bags over the four computers. I asked her if she was doing that to keep them dust-free. She said, "*No. I figured if I don't see them, I don't have to use them.*"

After that, I started getting it that we need to be realistic about what we teach teachers about technology, especially if they're not ready for it or don't have enough resources or are scared to use the technology.

There has to be a purpose for professional development, and it needs to be relevant and meaningful for them. I'm still glad I made the guides but decided the next time I created materials for any workshop, they had to be based on requests and identified needs. They had to be relevant to what teachers recognized as a need and what their students were learning.

Teachers usually start the profession with hope and expectations for their students and their classrooms. Reality hits them after a few days. We might have too many kids in our class, kids that are compliant or that have behavior problems, kids with poor test scores, etc. This is true for most people starting any profession. Teachers not only do their job, but they are also held accountable and responsible for their students (clients) to learn. We hope that we make a difference and have high expectations, but we fear they can become unrealistic expectations.

In my podcast, many educators have shared with me that they started college in a completely different career and then changed to education. Some like me started different careers and then found teaching later in life. Some teachers are spreading their wings as Edupreneurs. Others have shared how they started outside businesses to do while they teach, such as writing books, outside consulting, starting a podcast, or a radio show. I've talked to friends and neighbors who were struggling in their current jobs or some who retired and were not sure what's next for them. It's interesting who has reached out to me trying to figure out HOW they will find their WHY.

 He who has a WHY to live for can bear almost any HOW."

— Friedrich Nietzsche

You may find that your organization's vision may not align with your WHY. Reflect on the following questions:

- Can I continue working here even though I don't believe in my organization's vision?
- How can I find a way to develop my passion and stay with this organization?
- What can I do differently that is more aligned with my WHY?

Activity: Describe Your Feelings

One activity that Sinek writes about is how, when someone shares a story, the story is less important than how the person felt about what happened. I believe you still want the person to tell their story. That is why I started this book by asking you to tell your backstory and then to describe you as the main character in your story. I needed to learn more about what Sinek mentioned as the connection to feelings and how we feel about something or someone else who might be more powerful than ourselves. I adapted this activity for educators and others who are searching for their own purpose. I use the following questions when coaching someone who seems to be lost, who has a concern about something that happened to them, or is searching for their WHY. You can ask yourself or a partner these questions when you bring up something in your story that is impacting you.

Questions to uncover your feelings:

- When that happened, how did you feel?
- Was there anyone else who saw what happened?
- How did this experience affect you?

Questions to take your feelings deeper:

- What did you mean when you said _____?

- You say what happened made you feel _____.
  Explain.
- Have you ever felt that way before? What happened that
  caused that feeling?
- What makes this story special to you?

Reflect on your answers to the questions.

Consider your story and the feelings you had about that story. Did they bring up what you believe is you and your purpose? You may have an idea of your WHY. The next activity is for you to put down what you think your WHY, WHAT, and HOW is now. You can always come back and change this.

Activity: Starting with your WHY using the Golden Circle

Fill out the second column answering the questions the best you can. You may find that what you write now may change later when you discover more about you. You can update this as many times that work for you.

Why = The Purpose What do you believe? What makes your heart sing?	
What = The Goal What is your desired result to reach your purpose?	
How = The Process What are the specific actions you take to realize your Why?	

Activity: Draft your WHY statement

Your WHY statement is about your contribution that makes an impact on others. I had to think about my WHY in a completely different way when I thought of it that way. I adapted the activity from Simon Sinek's book, *Find the WHY*.

My contribution = stories with strategies and a process

My impact = inspire others to tell their stories

Here's how I might write my WHY statement:

To share stories, strategies, and a process so that I can inspire others to tell their stories.

To write your WHY statement, answer the following:

My contribution =_____

My impact = _____

Fill out the following WHY statement:

To _____ *[contribution]* **so that**
_____ *[impact]*.

This is your draft WHY statement. We will be coming back to review and update your WHY statement at the end of this book.

Questions to Ponder

- How are you learning through your WHAT?
- What do you do to bear almost any HOW?
- What thoughts do you have about your WHY statement?
- What feelings do you have when you think about your WHY?

Wonderings

Teachers and probably most of us were taught the WHAT and the HOW. We probably didn't know the WHY or even felt that we could ask why we were doing what we were told to do. Each of us is more than our profession. We have a variety of aspects of our lives. There might be times when you wanted to ask WHY but didn't have the confidence to do that. Now you can.

I've had several careers, interesting diversions, difficult struggles, but each challenge has helped me learn more about me. These were just different pathways to find me and my WHY even though I'm still learning it through my WHAT and HOW. All of us are here for a reason. We may know it or may have no clue what our purpose is, but it's there. We just have to explore, investigate, challenge, and be open to learning new things along our journey.

 When you know your WHY, you'll know your way."

— Michael Hyatt

* * *

If you are looking for additional resources and more about this chapter, go to:

- the book study questions, go to https://barbarabray.net
- digital resources, go to http://bit.ly/defineyourwhy-digital
- discussions on Twitter, use the hashtag #defineyourWHY

WHY GO WITH YOUR STRENGTHS, SKILLS, AND DISPOSITIONS?

Some folks have dozens of reasons why they cannot do what they want to when all they need is one..."

— LEWIS PUGH

Identifying Your Strengths

It is easy to give up when something is difficult. We tend to focus on things that are quick or easy to keep us from doing something we need to do. How do you create opportunities to do what you do best every day, even if it is difficult?

Gallup uses the CliftonStrengths Report for the workplace and in education to determine if the culture values a strength-based culture. They surveyed more than 10 million people on engagement at work on how positive and productive they are at work. Only one third "strongly agreed."

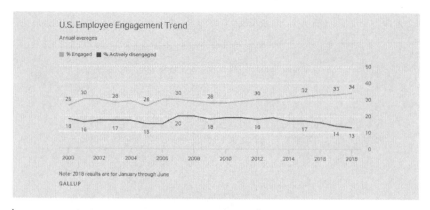

Fig. 4.1 Gallup U.S. Employee Engagement Trend

Workplaces that will win in the future require a change in strategy today. At the core of that strategy sits a focus on strengths and a culture that focuses on continual growth and improvement among everyone in the organization. Based on Gallup's study of human strengths, they created a language of the 34 most common themes using the Clifton StrengthsFinder assessment to help people discover and describe those themes (Rath, 2007).

 Everybody is a genius. But if you judge a fish by its ability to climb a tree, it will live its whole life thinking it is stupid."

— ALBERT EINSTEIN

Achiever	Activator	Adaptability	Analytical	Arranger	Belief	Command
Communication	Competition	Connectedness	Consistency	Context	Deliberative	Developer
Discipline	Empathy	Focus	Futuristic	Harmony	Ideation	Includer
Individualization	Input	Intellection	Learner	Maximizer	Positivity	Relator
Responsibility	Restorative	Self-Assurance	Significance	Strategic	Woo	

Table 4.1: 34 Themes in the Clifton StrengthsFinder

My top 5 from the list above are *Positivity, Learner, Empathy, Achiever, and Futuristic.*

You can try to choose your top five strengths from the list above on your own to get more details about each of the themes. You can get the book StrengthsFinder 2.0 (Rath, 2007) or go online to Strengths-Finder 2.0. https://www.gallup.com/press/176429/strengthsfinder.asp

You can also take their test to understand where you fit under the four domains (Strategic Thinking, Executing, Influencing, Relationship Building) at the GallupStrengthsCenter.

https://www.gallupstrengthscenter.com/home/en-us/cliftonstrengths-themes-domains

There is a free High5 test (https://high5test.com/) that asks you 100 questions (takes about 15 minutes) to determine your top five strengths. These are similar but different themes than those identified through the Strengths Finder. My top five from the High5 seem helpful and about right for me. Here is the report I received:

1. **Optimist:** Your objective is to bring a positive spirit. If there is someone believing that the glass is half-full instead of half-empty—then it's you. Whether it's a work project or a daily situation—you always manage to find a way to make everything more exciting. You inject enthusiasm into people and that's why they love to be around with you. Sure, there are people who don't buy your positivity—but could it set you back? No way! Your optimism simply would not allow it!

2. **Coach:** Your objective is to develop people's potential. Contrary to what others might think, you believe that every person has the potential for development—there is always space to grow. You perceive it as a personal mission to help others utilize their potential and to experience success. As a result, you look for ways to facilitate their learning process—from challenging their thoughts in a discussion to creating environments that would facilitate the learning process.

3. **Deliverer:** Your objective is to take responsibility. If there is a person who is emotionally bound to follow through on all

promises—then it's you. Your strong ethical principles do not let you to simply write missteps off on excuses and rationalizations. It holds true no matter how small or large is the issue you are dealing with. Your name and reputation depend on you being responsible for your commitments.

4. **Believer:** Your objective is to believe and to do 'the right thing.' Of course, 'the right thing' differs from person to person, but one thing is true—you have a certain set of values that you are not ready to compromise. Moreover, these values are like a compass guiding you, providing a direction and giving your life meaning and satisfaction. You believe that money is not the ultimate measure of success. Some people call you the person of purpose. It makes you very trustworthy and reliable in any environment.

5. **Brainstormer:** Your objective is to come up with new concepts and ideas. It's not even your objective—it's your way of life. You are constantly on the lookout to connect unconnectable things and to find new perspectives on familiar challenges. Whenever a new idea comes into your mind, you literally lit up like a light bulb. New angles, approaches, and perspectives no matter how contrary or bizarre give you an endless source of energy. As a result, others might see you as an innovative person willing to turn the world around and resort to you if they need some 'out of the box' ideas.

Activity: Reflect on your Top 5 Strengths

Choose or identify your top four or five strengths. You may want to see how you are using those strengths in your current situation.

- Write in your journal about your top strengths and reflect on why you see yourself with those strengths.
- Ask yourself how you are using them now. If you are not using them, why not?

- How would you like to use them in the future?

These are your strengths, and you may find others later because the world is changing, and so are you. No matter who you are or what you do, the world is changing, which has disrupted how we live, work, play, and learn now. This was when I started doing more research about the history and the future of learning and work.

 Look closely at the present you are constructing: it should look like the future you are dreaming."

— ALICE WALKER

Future of Learning and Work: The Industrial Revolutions

Each of the Industrial Revolutions disrupted where and how we lived, how we worked, and almost everything, including the economy, business, banking, and government. Education has been impacted, but "school" hasn't changed that much.

The **1st Industrial Revolution** starting around 1760 involved the transition to new manufacturing processes in Europe and the United States from an agrarian and handicraft economy to one dominated by industry and machine manufacturing. There was the emergence of mechanization, extraction of coal, and the invention of the steam engine. This brought about the development of railroads, which expanded travel, moving materials, and the growth of cities.

The **2nd Industrial Revolution** starting around 1870 involved the emergence of new technological advancements of electricity, the telegraph, telephone, radio, and the invention and manufacturing of the automobile and airplanes. These were made possible by mass production in the factory model.

The **3rd Industrial Revolution** starting around 1969 involved the emergence of nuclear energy and the rise of electronics with the transistor and microprocessor, which led to the development of computers and telecommunications. Miniaturizing opened the door to biotechnology, space research, automation, and robots.

The **4th Industrial Revolution**, where we are now, involves digitization where we build a virtual world in the cloud, data analysis, artificial intelligence (AI), virtual reality (VR), smart cities, wind, sun, and geothermal energy, and industrial cybersecurity all in an interconnected global system (Rouquet, 2017).

Past Industrial Revolutions have forced society to undergo major adaptations from rural agricultural societies to urban, industrial societies, and then to post-industrial societies dealing with the loss of traditional industries and sources of employment. Societies change as technology changes. Now we are noticing how everything is being disrupted. The 4th Industrial Revolution is changing how we live, how we work, how the economy works, and how we are governed. The current workforce is already feeling the heat. What does that mean for jobs in the future? Here are several predictions of possible job loss in the future.

- Translating languages (by 2024)
- Driving a truck (by 2027)
- Working in retail (by 2031)
- Writing a bestselling book (by 2049)
- Working as a surgeon (by 2053)

Pause/Think/Reflect
Do any of the predictions for jobs lost shock you?
Do you think the predictions can happen?
What are your concerns about any of these?

Machines and artificial intelligence (AI) are already spreading rapidly with self-driving cars, software that responds to customer service inquiries, and robots that flip hamburgers and check store inventory. Virtual reality and robotics are used during surgery. Ingestible remote-controlled robots perform procedures from inside out. Contact lenses use the Internet where you can see subtitles in any language, remember names, and get biographies. Construction is using 3D printing to build a whole house in 24 hours.

Artificial intelligence and automation will create more jobs than they replace, according to a new report entitled *"The Future of Jobs"* from the World Economic Forum (WEF). According to the report, by 2022, automation will displace about 75 million jobs worldwide (Melendez, 2018).

On the other hand, if or when technology destroys jobs, they will create an estimated 133 million new jobs. The predictions come from surveys sent to more than 300 major employers around the world. By 2025, the WEF report predicts that humans will do just 48% of the hours of work done by humans or machines.

Maybe data is the new oil. What skills will be needed?

People will need to understand how to manage data, use powerful tools to bring data together from multiple sources, organize proper storage, keep data secure, understand the trends and predictions using data, and apply academic processes and tools that enable the creation of predictive models (Cantrell, 2018).

Since privacy and security is a concern in this digital age, a new position that is growing and in need now is the Director of Privacy and Policy. Just imagine the skills kids could be acquiring now for this position.

 We live our lives responding to a world that we know and understand, but no longer exists."

— EDDIE OBENG

Preparing for Our Future

With the information about job loss and the need for different skills, there is an urgent need to improve educational systems, create safety nets for those displaced, and support an ecosystem for lifelong learners that includes telecommuting opportunities and freelancing in the gig economy. What all of this means is that people will need to know their why for learning new skills throughout their lives. Rachelle Dene Poth is an author, writer, speaker, and keynoter, and she wrote *The Future is Now.* I invited Rachelle to share her ideas about preparing students for our future.

* * *

How can we prepare for our future?
By Rachelle Dene Poth @Rdene915

We cannot accurately predict what the future of work or the future of learning will look like, so how do we prepare our students and ourselves, for five, ten, or more years down the road? By connecting with other educators, actively learning about emerging trends in education, we will have the best access to the information we need. It has never been more important for educators to be in constant pursuit of knowledge and to consistently engage in challenging learning opportunities. We have now entered a new era of education and must prepare ourselves and our students for the future. *But how?*

- Be intentional in planning experiences that will foster the skills of adaptability, resilience, and persistence.
- Seek learning opportunities that will promote the development of skills such as problem-solving, critical thinking, collaboration, and communication.

- Understand the new trends impacting education and work (e.g., AI, AR/VR, gig economy, entrepreneurship).
- Create ways for students to become risk-takers as they design their own learning journeys.

As educators, we are in a unique position to not only enhance learning for our students but to challenge ourselves as we move toward the future. Schools today should focus on providing opportunities for students to explore their interests, to solve big problems, to connect globally, and to design their own learning paths. To prepare our students for the "real world," they need to see how the world works, identify challenges that exist, and help find solutions. Today we are facing new ideas and even uncertainties because of new technologies.

Artificial intelligence is part of our everyday existence and we must learn how to use AI for our benefit.

We must focus on the purpose. Learning how AI will impact education and the world of work in the future will empower students to be more engaged in learning. It can lead to higher-level thinking and discussions about the impact of AI and the ethics surrounding AI in education and its use in the world. With an estimate of close to 40% of the jobs being replaced by artificial intelligence in the future, we need to understand how these technologies will impact our future. Our students may end up creating the AI and developing the technologies that we will be using in the not-too-distant future.

What skills do all students need to develop regardless of what the future holds in terms of education and work?

Students must learn how to communicate, to collaborate, to problem-solve, and to explore their interests. They need opportunities to engage in more real-world experiences like project or place-based learning, where they can identify needs in their community and brainstorm ways to help others. These skills will prove beneficial regardless of what the future "job" may be for students.

When we support students in setting goals, learning to self-assess, engaging in more independent work, and developing time management skills, they will develop skills that they will need in the future regardless of what they ultimately decide to do. While the look and format of schools and education may change, the skills they need to acquire will prepare them to face any challenges that arise in a constantly changing workplace.

Blog and Website "Learning as I Go: https://rdene915.com/
The host of #formativechat – Every Monday evening at 7:30 pm ET
Both of my books are linked through http://bit.ly/Pothbooks
Book: (Dene Poth, R. Future is Now. 2019)

Podcast Episode #70: Taking Risks and Learning from Students Taking the Lead with Rachelle Dene Poth http://bit.ly/episode70-poth

* * *

Skills and Dispositions Needed for 2030

Forty-six percent of U.S. employers are having a difficult time hiring because they cannot find the people with the skills that they actually need in the workforce. This is explained in more detail at Discover More is part of a Build Your Future (BYF) article online on minding the gap: (http://discover.byf.org/mind-the-gap-why-the-skills-gap-in-construction-is-a-critical-issue/).

The push for a four-year degree is not filling the skills gap that the world is facing. In the Future of Jobs Report, the World Economic Forum (www.weforum.org) shares the Top 10 Skills needed over a 15 year period along with data from The Future of Skills (https://futureskills.pearson.com/).

in 2015	in 2020	in 2030
1. Complex Problem Solving	1. People Management	1. Judgment & Decision Making
2. Coordinating with Others	2. Complex Problem Solving	2. Fluency of Ideas
3. People Management	3. Critical Thinking	3. Active Learning
4. Critical Thinking	4. Creativity	4. Learning Strategies
5. Negotiation	5. Coordinating with Others	5. Originality
6. Quality Control	6. Emotional Intelligence	6. System Evaluation
7. Service Orientation	7. Judgment & Decision Making	7. Deductive Reasoning
8. Judgment & Decision Making	8. Service Orientation	8. Complex Problem Solving
9. Active Listening	9. Negotiation	9. Systems Analysis
10. Creativity	10. Cognitive Flexibility	10. Monitoring

Table 4.2 Skills from 2015 to 2030

You may not see how the skills employers are looking for have changed from 2015 to 2020, but are we teaching the skills listed in the list under 2015? Project-based learning (PBL) activities do encourage working on complex problems and coordinating with others. Yet, are we putting too much focus on content instead of context? If you collaborate on a project, you need to know how to determine the best person for the task, support each other, brainstorm ideas, negotiate, and possibly compromise on issues.

Pause/Think/Reflect
Did you learn these skills and experience these activities as a learner or a teacher? Are you coordinating with others to design real-world projects for an authentic audience?

Let's think about 2030 and the skills that this chart is projecting people will need by then. Now consider that kindergarteners (five- or six-year-olds) will be 10th or 11th graders by 2030. We cannot wait until they are in high school to build these skills. We need to start early, maybe in Pre-K, to prepare our kids for their future. They need these skills while they go through school and for what they will need in their lives. The world is changing way too fast.

With disruption driving workforce changes, human, business and digital skills were now considered foundational for the new economy, with an 'ability to learn' seen as a graduate's most valuable asset. LinkedIn Asia Pacific Senior Director Jason Laufer said the company used information from its 650 million members and 1.3 trillion bytes of data to predict future work trends. He said the world had changed, with people now working to learn, not vice versa.

 Roughly 65 percent of jobs for the next generation don't exist today but focusing on soft skills will help you get the hard skills," he said. *"Our biggest learning adventure is to 'unlearn' – getting rid of our biases to learning new things."*

— Knowledge is Power: Skilling Students for the
Future

Activity: Reflecting on Skills and Dispositions

Consider the following questions as you reflect on the different skills we currently teach and have now, the skills gap, and what skills dispositions people will need for the future. Add your reflections to your journal.

- Have we been teaching the skills listed for 2015?
- When you look at the skills for 2020, what do you see was added? What was removed? Why?
- How early should we teach these skills?
- What do these skills and dispositions mean for you and your future?

Entrepreneurship

I started thinking about the skills all learners will need and thought of Dan Jackson. I am connected to Dan on Twitter and was interested in his #runandrants (sharing a video around a topic you are passionate about) and wanted to learn more about his story. I am fortunate that I had a conversation on my podcast, Episode #81, with Dan, and found out that education was his second career. His background in sales and marketing led him to teach International Business and Marketing classes. His goal, *"To nurture student's curiosity and creativity through building culture and community one classroom at a time,"* developed into his non-profit ASaP (Applied Synergies Partnership). Dan was the perfect person to add a story about entrepreneurship.

* * *

Giving Students What They Need
By Dan Jackson

For some years now, my vision has been for all learners of all ages to wake up every day and to look forward to going to school. This was brought about by the bi-annual Gallup survey that has come to be known as the Student Engagement Cliff. The study indicates a waning interest in school from the time a student enters secondary school to the time they graduate. Fully two-thirds of high school upper-classmen are not engaged! Our young learners deserve to be turned on by their learning, not bored and stressed!

A prescription I spoke of at my TEDxRaleigh Talk was to encourage students to take rigorous and relevant courses that engaged their minds and equip them with the skills that they would need in the Life After, The Life After High School. We all should develop a love of lifelong learning. Integral ingredients for this are curiosity, initiative, research & analysis, adaptability, and entrepreneurism. Many of our young learners have schooled out of them these key traits and skills once they enter middle school. The drive for "college-ready" creates proficient test-takers, not thinkers, doers and innovators.

Experiential Entrepreneurship Education is a balanced blend of knowledge acquisition, learning how to apply that knowledge to the solution of a real-world problem and the intentional development of skills critical to our future success as an economy and a country. The emphasis is on learning from experiences and events, not textbooks and tests. This is delivered in a supportive, free-thinking environment where overcoming setbacks and managing obstacles is a whole-class effort. One student said,

"We are not learning out of books, we are learning from experience which will eventually help us later in life and we will remember it better. We are judged on how well we can complete something not upon our memory."

Semester-long Project Based Learning creates a significant investment made by the learner that creates a long-term return, especially when compared to the more frequently used "unit projects." Different skills are developed at different times, and often multiple abilities are working in concert to deliver the final product. How long-term projects help might best be answered by the students themselves:

"Our original ideas have been shut down, revised, and redone multiple times. . . . . Along with the help of Mr. Jackson, we have been able to think of spectacular ways to attack our problems so that we can turn them into actual ideas and things we do for our project."

"Unlike other classes, instead of just learning a concept and testing on it, we've taken what we have learned and applied it to our business plan."

It is important to me that more instructors deliver experiences and events and not rely heavily on textbooks to prepare our emerging leaders. Our non-profit, Applied Synergies Partnership (ASaP) intends to create and deliver workshops to other educators who wish to give kids what they truly deserve. We need more young learners saying things like,

"All in all, I always feel that at the end of the day that I am learning more in this class than any other course I have taken by far. It is providing such great opportunities and areas for growth and improvement. . . This class isn't trying to just get numbers out of me and into a book and then move onto the next numbered student. This class really is what I've been looking for a long time."

Website: https://appliedsynergypartnership.weebly.com/
Twitter: @Mind_on_ASaP
Podcast Episode #81: Providing a S.P.I.R.I.T.E.D. Environment Where Students Thrive
http://bit.ly/episode81-jackson
Gallup Student Poll https://www.gallup.com/education/233537/gallup-student-poll.aspx

* * *

Fixed vs. Growth Mindset

With the workforce changing rapidly before our eyes, we will see careers and jobs going away sooner than later. Today's workers will need to develop new skills and dispositions before they lose their jobs. This involves dispositions that are a person's inherent qualities of mind and character. You have to be willing to change. If it is inevitable that certain jobs will be lost, then we need to include mindset activities that encourage having an attitude of gratitude and developing a growth mindset.

Based on decades of research exploring achievement and success, Stanford University psychologist Carol Dweck developed the theory of a growth mindset as opposed to a fixed mindset.

In a **fixed mindset**, people believe their basic qualities, like their intelligence or talent, are simply fixed traits. They spend their time documenting their intelligence or talent instead of developing them. They also believe that talent alone creates success—without effort. They're wrong.

In a **growth mindset**, people believe that their most basic abilities can be developed through dedication and hard work—brains and talent are just the starting point. This view creates a love of learning and a resilience that is essential for great accomplishment. Virtually all great people have had these qualities. (Source: https://mindsetonline.com/whatisit/about/)

Activity: Changing Mindsets

| https://youtu.be/42E2fAWM6rA

- Watch the video "Lost Generation" above (2 minutes).
- Explore where you feel fixed or growth mindset appears.
- Share the video with someone else and discuss what you found out about how the future changes depending on the mindsets we choose to adopt.

Pause/Reflect/Journal
What happens when we change our mindset?

This concept of a growth mindset brings up the idea of "upskilling" since people are moving up and changing by unlearning, relearning, and developing new skills. Check out this article on transforming careers, "A Movement to Transform West Virginia Coal Miners into Beekeepers is Great for the Planet" (Humphries, 2019).

Interests, Aspirations, and What We are Good At

All of us have interests and things we are good at. In fact, people have probably told us we're good at this or that. Unfortunately, many of us believe we are not good at things and make excuses not to push ourselves. If we change our minds and use the concept of YET, it can change our mindset.

We may say we cannot do _____, but we need to add YET at the end. I wasn't ready for even adding YET. When you are trained to do one thing, and that one thing is no longer available, it's scary. This is where I was when I had to change careers. I had a fixed mindset that I was trained to be a dental hygienist and spent many years perfecting my skills just for that career.

When I was recuperating for four months, I didn't believe in myself and that I could change. When I was hurt and realized I needed to discover a new me, I only focused on the pain and suffering I was going through. I was having my own "pity party." My doctor was concerned and suggested seeking help from a therapist and a career counselor. Through therapy and discovering me, I realized I had more skills than I knew. I was already teaching and had taken different self-assessments about me like Myers-Briggs. I read many self-help books, including *The Color of My Parachute*. I guess I was searching for meaning and trying to find my WHY then. After I started teaching kids and then teaching adults, I realized I wasn't the only one trying to find their WHY. When I began my coaching program with My eCoach in 2000 and started the train-the-coach programs, I used different inventories and assessments with coaches to support teachers and their students.

Through multiple derivatives of the first inventory, I created the "Me as a Learner" form for my coaching and workshops on personalized learning, developing agency, and Define Your WHY. The suggestions educators gave me that they got from their students was to simplify the questions for Part One to make them more open-ended.

Activity: Me as a Learner - Part One

Fill out "Me as a Learner" Part One to get to know you better.

I am really good at...

For fun, I like to...

I am really curious about...

I would like to learn how to...

One thing unique or special about me is...

I want to make a difference about...

Circle any of the words below that best represent you:
Funny, Intense, Strong, Perfectionist, Out-of-Box Thinker, Social, Fearful, Curious, Talkative, Independent, Artistic, Calm, Introvert, Geek, Silly, Risk-Taker, Friendly, Listener, Thinker, Musical, Extrovert, Focused, Creative, Determined, Stubborn, Intelligent, Shy, Innovative, Nerdy, Follower, Leader, Bubbly, Quiet, Talented, Athletic, Loner, Mediator, Hugger

Add any other words to describe you if not listed above:

Keep these questions with your journal to reflect on and use later.

Self-Doubt and Belonging

Even though you may have filled out "Me as a Learner," you may doubt that you can change. You may not feel a sense of belonging. I had self-doubts on what I could achieve in school and didn't feel I belonged. Every time we moved to a new place and a new school, I learned how to work the system so I could get through school. I had to. My file and label followed me. This happens to many kids who believe that they cannot make it through school, so they fumble through.

What do you do if your child fails first grade? The system can label your child. That label then defines your child. That happened to Lois Letchford's son, Nicholas, and Lois decided to change the label and his mindset to overcome the odds, so he believed in himself. I asked Lois if she could share their story.

* * *

Overcoming the Odds
By Lois Letchford

In 1994, my son, Nicholas Letchford, failed first grade. During this year, he bit his fingernails and wet his pants every day, while his teacher shouted at him for failing to follow directions. At the end of the year, he was tested, revealing he could only read ten words, had no strengths, and had an IQ "just above intellectually impaired."

In 1995, my husband, a professor, took a six-month study leave in Oxford, England, from our home in Australia. I used this opportunity to work one-on-one with Nicholas. Using books called *Success for All,* we failed miserably. Nicholas appeared to have no memory for words, letters, or sounds. But then, I was given incredible advice: "Lois, make learning fun."

Faced with a blank slate, I reassessed the situation and began thinking out of the box—and our classroom changed immediately. I wanted to engage Nicholas in the CVC words (consonant-vowel-consonant words), so I began writing simple poetry. Together we illustrated it. And, as my poetry grew, the content changed. The "oo" sounds brought words such as cook, look, and book. In my poetry, I focused on Captain James Cook, the last of the great explorers. Nicholas asked: "Who came before Captain Cook? Who came before Columbus?" I knew these inquisitive questions did not come from a child with a low IQ.

Unexpectedly tapping into Nicholas's curiosity led to his love of learning—revealing hidden strengths testing couldn't show. This changed his—and my—life. This life-changing memory helped me see reading as being a complex set of interactions, with teaching decoding as just one component.

Nicholas's label, Specific Learning Disability, put him into a category of "garden-variety" of poor learners. No particular reason for his failure, he was just not smart. His reading teacher focused on teaching decoding—his weakness.

My son went from failing first grade, tested to have a low IQ, to graduating with a Ph.D. from Oxford University. Our story itself is amazing, yet his journey depended on circumstances. Never should a child have to move anywhere to become a reader. Becoming a reading specialist teaching children who failed various reading programs helped me reinforce the power of the teacher and their *mindset*. I wrote my book to say, "We simply must teach children to read—irrespective of any label."

CONTACT INFO: Lois Letchford Lois@LetchfordLois.com
BOOK LINK: Reversed: A Memoir available wherever books are sold. (Letchford, 2018)
WEBSITE: https://www.loisletchford.com/

Podcast Episode #95: Overcoming the Odds for Struggling Learners
http://bit.ly/episode95-letchford

* * *

 Believe in yourself, your abilities and your own potential. Never let self-doubt hold you captive. You are worthy of all that you dream of and hope for."

— Roy Bennett

In her TEDx Talk, Ulcca Joshi Hansen advocates for an approach to learning that focuses on supporting the development needs of young people. Her experiences as the child of two immigrants have informed her beliefs around what it means to provide an "equitable education" for all students. Hansen truly believes that this sense of belonging and purpose immersed with education is the only foundation strong enough to build a life that is meaningful by breaking down the barriers of the traditional way of learning and teaching and replacing reading, writing, and arithmetic with three new R's: relationship, relevance, and reintegration.

| https://youtu.be/g7zno4iQRFA

Questions to Ponder

- Why do we need to continue to learn new skills throughout our lives? What skills will you want to develop?
- What jobs do you believe will be lost, and by when? What new jobs do you think will take their place?
- What did you find out about yourself that surprised you in "Me as a Learner" Part One?
- Have you ever changed from a fixed mindset to a growth mindset? What happened?

Wonderings

I know AI, VR, and automation will take over more and more jobs, and I wonder if displaced workers will have opportunities to be retrained and upskilled. What will happen to entitlements like Social Security, Medicare, and Medicaid? I am concerned about people who have worked their whole lives and may not afford to stay in their homes or community. Because the world is changing and impacting everything we do and how we live, we have no idea what this means for us, our families, friends, and most of the people in our world. I believe that we can be proactive and start rethinking, relearning, and redesigning how we can be retrained or retrain others on new skills we will need for their future now. We have to because the future is getting closer every day.

* * *

If you are looking for additional resources and more about this chapter, go to:

- the book study questions, go to https://barbarabray.net
- digital resources, go to http://bit.ly/defineyourwhy-digital
- discussions on Twitter, use the hashtag #defineyourWHY

WHY USE UNIVERSAL DESIGN FOR LEARNING (UDL)?

Universal Design for Learning (UDL)

Universal Design for Learning (UDL), developed by David Rose and Anne Meyer from CAST (Center for Applied Special Technology), provides suggestions on how learners can reduce barriers and maximize their learning. When I first learned about UDL, the UDL Principles started with the WHAT. After 2014, Rose and Meyer co-authored "Universal Design for Learning: Theory and Practice," demonstrating why UDL starts with engagement. Because this made sense to me, I changed the direction of my work from the WHAT to the WHY to represent the changes. I believe UDL can support all learners of any age who want a framework for learning and who want to define their WHY and learn on purpose.

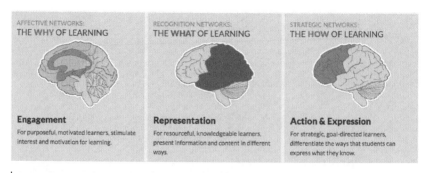

| Fig. 5.1 Universal Design for Learning Principles

Universal Design for Learning (UDL) by CAST

(www.cast.org)

The three UDL principles:

- *Multiple Means of Engagement* = The **WHY** of Learning
- *Multiple Means of Representation* = The **WHAT** of Learning
- *Multiple Means of Action and Expression* = The **HOW** of Learning

I love that UDL starts with the WHY when we are motivated to learn what we are interested in and passionate about. I like the idea of being curious about who we are as learners. Why not ask our own WHY to ourselves about how we learn?

Pause/Think/Reflect
Why are we engaged or not engaged in learning?
Why do we need to be motivated to want to learn?
Why would we want to become independent and self-directed?

UDL Guidelines

The UDL Guidelines at http://udlguidelines.cast.org/ provide a set of suggestions that can be applied to reduce barriers and maximize learning opportunities for all learners. Below is a shortened version of the structure organized both horizontally and vertically. The Guidelines are organized across the table according to the three UDL principles starting with Engagement.

	Multiple Means of Engagement	Multiple Means of Representation	Multiple Means of Action and Expression
	Providing options for	*Providing options for*	*Providing options for*
Access	Recruiting Interest	Perception	Physical Action
	The "access" row includes the guidelines that suggest ways to increase access to the learning goal by recruiting interest and by offering options for perception and physical action.		
Build	Sustaining Effort and Persistence	Language and Symbols	Expression and Communication
	The "build" row includes the guidelines that suggest ways to develop effort and persistence, language and symbols, and expression and communication.		
Internalize	Self-Regulation	Comprehension	Executive Functions
	The "internalize" row includes the guidelines that suggest ways to empower learners through self-regulation, comprehension, and executive function.		
	WHY of Learning	**WHAT of Learning**	**HOW of Learning**

| **Table. 5.1 UDL Guidelines Structure**

The options scaffold down the table from "access" to "build" and then to "internalize" to develop "expert learners" who are resourceful and knowledgeable, strategic and goal-directed, purposeful, and motivated. The table below provides only a few examples of the checkpoints.

Provide multiple means of **Engagement**	Provide multiple means of **Representation**	Provide multiple means of **Action and Expression**
Learners are purposeful and motivated by... • Optimizing individual choice and autonomy • Minimizing threats and distractions • Fostering collaboration and community • Facilitating personal coping skills and strategies	Learners are resourceful and knowledgeable by... • Offering ways to customize the display of information • Offering alternative auditory and visual information • Illustrating through multiple media • Activating or supplying background knowledge	Learners are strategic and goal-directed by... • Optimizing access to tools and resources • Using multiple tools for communication & composition • Guiding goal-setting • Facilitating managing information and resources • Monitoring progress
Affective Networks The "WHY" of Learning	Recognition Networks The "WHAT" of Learning	Strategic Networks The "HOW" of Learning

Table. 5.2 UDL Guidelines with Examples of the Checkpoints

The UDL Guidelines at http://udlguidelines.cast.org/ provide opportunities for you to learn more about how the principles are expanded in the Guidelines. The bulleted list below each Guideline includes the corresponding checkpoints that go deeper by linking to strategies and research for more detailed suggestions.

Activity: Go Deeper with the Checkpoints

Review the Guidelines and the checkpoints. Choose one checkpoint for each UDL Principle and identify one strategy for each UDL Principle to support your learning. Provide a rationale for why you chose this strategy for you.

Here is an example to go deeper:

Multiple Means of Engagement	
Checkpoint	1. Strategy to support your learning
7.1 Optimize individual choice and autonomy	Provide as much discretion and autonomy as possible by providing choices in the tools used for information gathering or production. *My rationale is because I am finding new tools and apps to support researching, curating, and designing that go beyond my current tools. I need to explore more apps and try them to see if they will be more effective for my work.*

Now it's your turn.

Multiple Means of Engagement	
Checkpoint	1. Strategy to support your learning
Multiple Means of Representation	
Checkpoint	2. Strategy to support your learning
Multiple Means of Action and Expression	
Checkpoint	3. Strategy to support your learning

Table. 5.3 Go Deeper with the Checkpoints

After you write the three strategies, consider and reflect in your journal how you plan to use and adapt these strategies with something you are learning right now.

Finding My WHY for Learning

I decided to explore the UDL Guidelines from my perspective as a learner before sharing this with others. I know that I need to be motivated first about something new that I want or need to learn. I'm kind of busy. There has to be a reason or purpose for my learning. When I thought about this, I got why UDL starts with Multiple Means of Engagement. This is what makes learning personal for me. It is not about what someone else teaches me unless that is when I need to learn specific information. I first have to be interested in what I want to learn. I believe that most people need to be motivated to want to learn.

Universal Design was developed to make places, actions, and materials accessible for people who may need a ramp instead of stairs or glasses to see. Universal Design for Learning was developed by CAST (Center for Accessible Special Technology) to reduce barriers and maximize learning. When you consider that the mouse was developed for alternative ways to input text or audible books for those who are blind, everyone can benefit from these tools. The UDL Guidelines were designed to scaffold learning strategies to support all learners.

Because of starting with the WHY instead of the WHAT, I needed to update the Part Two of "Me as a Learner" with new statements for Strengths, Competencies, Challenges, and Obstacles. I reached out to focus groups in the U.S., Canada, and New Zealand who use UDL and other inventories to understand how we learn best.

Activity: Me as a Learner Part Two

I appreciate the educators who piloted the "Me as a Learner" document with their students. From the feedback, we came up with new statements for each of the UDL principles. The current document is below. There are three sections reflecting statements in two columns: (1) Strengths and Competencies and (2) Challenges and Obstacles. For each section, check the boxes at the left for as many statements that can apply to you. Then circle only 10 in each section that you checked.

Table 5.4 Me as a Learner Part Two (3 tables)

How I Feel About Myself and Learning (Multiple Means of Engagement)

Strengths and Competencies	Challenges and Obstacles
I feel confident and motivated to want to learn.	I get discouraged and frustrated easily.
I get excited about learning new ideas.	I feel overwhelmed much of the time.
I learn from my mistakes and don't give up.	I worry too much.
I know what is important and what to do first.	I need things to be perfect.
I like to challenge myself to learn more.	I get bored fast and give up quickly.
I like working alone.	I don't expect to be successful.
I make friends easily.	I get anxious when the attention is on me.
I am lucky to have people who are there for me.	I feel I am not very creative.
I feel I'm really curious and creative.	I can't say what I'm thinking very well.
I have a good imagination.	I don't have very many friends.
I feel happy most of the time.	I sometimes pretend to know what I'm doing and fake it.
I can feel what someone else is feeling.	I cannot cope with many things at one time.
I am more engaged when doing what I like.	I joke around when working or learning.
I like working and playing with others.	I keep thinking about the bad things that happened.
I feel like I am a better leader than others.	I feel I don't always belong here.
I like who I am.	I'm not sure who I am supposed to be.

How I Process Information (Multiple Means of Representation)

Strengths and Competencies	Challenges and Obstacles
I understand what I read most of the time.	I have trouble seeing things that are far away..
I ask good questions when I need help.	I cannot hear well with background noise.
I can see or visualize what I hear or read.	I often do not understand what I read.
I know how to use maps and charts.	I read slowly or have to re-read the text.
I understand math symbols and concepts.	I cannot understand or read in English.
I learn more like a hands-on learner.	I have trouble focusing on one thing.
I can follow directions easily.	I often don't understand what others are telling me.
I think differently than others.	I am uncomfortable asking for help.
I can read and learn about using technology.	It is difficult to understand oral directions.
I learn better by working with others.	I have trouble following written directions.
I connect to ideas I already know.	I am confused about technology.
I learn content better that includes pictures.	I am not good at remembering things.
I believe I'm a good listener.	I cannot always find what I need online.
I enjoy learning new vocabulary words.	I have trouble understanding new vocabulary.
I have good problem-solving skills.	I need directions repeated often.
I have a good memory.	I don't understand why I cannot learn some things.
I enjoy listening to music when learning.	I am uncomfortable using technology online.

How I Demonstrate My Learning (Multiple Means of Action and Expression)

Strengths and Competencies	Challenges and Obstacles
I ask for help when I am working on a task.	It is hard for me to say what I am thinking.
I like drawing and using photos in my projects.	I feel anxious to speak in front of people.
I like to build things.	It is difficult to get started on a new activity.
I like to write essays, stories, poetry, or songs.	I can't take notes and listen at the same time.
I am good at organizing and planning.	I have messy handwriting.
I can draw what I am thinking.	I put off planning and finishing tasks.
I can manage information and resources.	I have a speech impairment.
I can explain things and retell a story well.	I don't like to study.
I notice and reflect on what I am learning.	I have trouble putting thoughts on paper.
I participate in group and class discussions.	I cannot speak or present in English.
I can create multimedia presentations.	I cannot organize my ideas very well.
I enjoy defending my position.	I have trouble taking notes for learning.
I like to show evidence of my learning.	I am not good at reflecting on what I learned.
I am good at telling stories.	I know what I read but cannot explain it well.
I use technology to communicate and create.	I cannot defend my position very well.
I enjoy using social media.	I am not good at drawing or illustrating.
I am good at problem-solving.	I do not feel good about setting goals.

Reflect on what you checked and circled for all three sections.

- Write in your journal a summary of what stands out about you that are your top five or six strengths and competencies.
- Write what stands out about you that are your top five or six challenges and obstacles.
- Reflect on the skills you have or those you wish you had based on what you found out about you.

Save this information to refer to later as you learn your WHY for learning. You may want to rethink your choices over time after you learn more about you.

The Learner Profile

I have met many teachers around the world who reached out to me to support their work with the Learner Profile. For over 15 years, I worked with special education teachers around the U.S. and learned about different tools and resources to enhance learning. I was constantly learning that what worked for special needs students worked for all students. Andelee Espinosa leads a talented team of six other special education teachers at Brookfield Central High School in Brookfield, Wisconsin. I really appreciate the feedback she gave me from what worked and what didn't work. I asked Andelee to share the story about the Learner Profile around one student and how it took the IEP process deeper. The Individualized Educational Plan (IEP) is a plan or program developed to ensure that a child who has a disability identified under the law and is attending an elementary or secondary educational institution receives specialized instruction and related services.

* * *

The Learner Profile Gives Voice and Develops the IEP
By Andelee Espinosa

Every year, I get a new class of freshman students on my special education caseload. I read their IEPs, and there are some similarities between all the students who, let's say, have needs in the area of reading. Each of them has something like "text-to-speech" to accommodate reading fluency needs. While I acknowledge this is an appropriate and highly effective accommodation for a student with fluency deficits, not every student prefers computer-generated audio. Yet, as soon as we write it into an IEP, the school needs to provide it whether a student prefers it or not.

I met Emma in her freshman year, and she had some strong

opinions about text-to-speech. She knew she could be distracted by technology, and listening to text from a laptop challenged her self-regulation skills. Her comprehension was impacted by the computer-generated voice, so she preferred to just take extra time to read to herself–sometimes out loud. Additionally, she did not prefer to take multiple-choice assessments on the computer because she couldn't mark the text up. However, every year at her IEP meeting, the adults in the room continually told her that she needed to use text-to-speech even though that wasn't her preference.

During the presentation of her Learner Profile, she explained to the room that extended time was her preference over text-to-speech and that hard copies of assessments allowed her to mark the text. The technology was hindering her application of the strategies she had learned, preferred, and utilized and made self-regulation difficult. The Learner Profile allowed her to organize her preferences in an organized manner and gave her a voice during the development of her IEP. She now effectively utilizes double time for assessments that require large amounts of reading and only uses audio recordings for novels.

Twitter Handle: @AndeleeEspinosa
Website: http://arespinosa.blogspot.com/
Episode #92: Creating Student Agency, Ownership, and Empowerment with Andelee Espinosa
http://bit.ly/episode92-espinosa

* * *

My Learner Profile

Universal Design for Learning (UDL) helped me to define my WHY for learning. Through Part One of "Me as a Learner," I was able to write about my interests, aspirations, and identify words that represented me as a learner. In Part Two, I identified statements that represented strengths, competencies, challenges, and obstacles in my learning.

I could see why UDL is important to start with the WHY of learning. We need a voice and choice, so we own our learning and focus on strengths to maximize our learning and to find strategies to reduce any barriers that may keep us from learning. We may all process that information differently. Consequently, this is why we need to know how we learn best. UDL helps us do that. I figured if I'm going to share UDL and this Learner Profile, I needed to see how it worked for me as a learner. I filled out the "Me as a Learner" form and created a summary. Below is a sample from my summary:

I feel confident and motivated to want to learn but at times have this need to be perfect. I'm realizing I don't know as much as I thought I did and don't like being called an "expert." I do like collaborating with others who want to become better learners and learn from others. I realized I was not focusing on what I'm passionate about and now wish to define my WHY so I can inspire others to define theirs.

For my profile, I added what I learned from "Me as a Learner" and what I came up with my strengths earlier in this chapter, along with ideas from the checkpoints. I added more descriptive words than what I came up with in Chapter 2 that others have said about me. I also added ways to address obstacles as wishes.

	Strengths and Competencies	Challenges and Wishes
Engagement	• I encourage positive thinking. • I can learn if I put my mind to it. • I enjoy collaborating with others.	• I need to spend more time on things I am passionate about. • I wish to define and share my WHY.
Representation	• I can connect to prior knowledge. • I use multiple formats to read and research information.	• I need text or video over oral directions. • I wish there was a better way to use visuals to present my ideas.
Action and Expression	• I take responsibility for any commitment or the task I take on. • I use and refer to a to-do list to stay on task.	• I need to put an action plan with tasks together to meet any goal. • I wish there was an app that connected all my tasks, to-dos, and reminders on my calendar and my iWatch.

Interests, Talents, Aspirations	Descriptive Words
Writing, Dancing, Designing, Gardening, Playing Games, Social Media, Storytelling Aspire to become a better writer and speaker	Curious, Creative, Kind, Silly, Risk-Taker, Connector, Independent, Collaborator, Leader, Storyteller, Designer, Strategist, Disruptor

Table. 5.5 Learner Profile

What I noticed is that when I started writing about my strengths and interests for engagement, it was all about purpose. Yet, I wasn't sure of my purpose. This was big for me. I've been focusing on making learning personal for years, and now I wasn't sure if that was my WHY.

When I added information about me, I saw me. I wanted to share it. I shared the learner profile with educators in focus groups and workshops and asked them how they would use this. So they filled it out and then shared what they found out about themselves with peers. I was concerned about sharing mine with you. When I asked someone what they thought about what I wrote, they asked me questions that led to some very interesting conversations. One teacher said that when I wrote that I wished to define my WHY, it helped her feel okay about not knowing her WHY and being vulnerable in front of others. She thought I knew everything. No one knows everything. I definitely do not feel like an expert. Every day I learn something new and am humbled by how much I don't know.

Pause/Think/Reflect

It's amazing how much we don't know what we don't know.

I offered only a few ideas for you to get an idea of how this process works. Putting my thoughts in writing helped me see what I was thinking. I needed to refine my purpose and spend more time on things I'm passionate about. That's number one. That's my WHY.

Pause/Think/Reflect

What are you passionate about and wish you could learn?

	Strengths	Challenges and Wishes
Engagement		
Representation		
Action and Expression		

Interests, Talents, Aspirations	Descriptive Words

Resources and Skills to be Future-Ready

To build my skills, I did some research on what I could use to better organize my thoughts and present my ideas. There are many apps available right at our fingertips. I reached out to my Personal Learning Network (PLN) for ideas about different apps that might meet my needs.

Tools and Apps	Learning Strategies	Skills and Competencies
PearDeck	Learners can answer questions and participate in discussions in interactive lessons, presentations, or slides at their own pace.	Presenting, designing, collaborating, assessing and monitoring progress
Flipgrid	Learners have a voice to create, participate, and collaborate with others in a video discussion platform.	Speaking, listening, and collaborating
Wakelet	Learners can curate, save, and share collections that include stories, videos, and blogs.	Organizing, curating, and collaborating
Book Creator	Learners incorporate their own text, images, audio, and video in an original story.	Creating, designing, and publishing to an authentic audience
Trello	Learners can create, participate, and collaborate in lists of cards and boards for project management.	Organizing, planning, tracking, and monitoring progress
Buncee	Learners can create visual representations, presentations, and media-rich content.	Designing, creating, communicating, collaborating, and publishing
My eCoach	Educators and others can create websites, blogs, surveys, and more and lead or participate in a team.	Creating, writing, surveying, collaborating, publishing, and coaching

Table 5.6 Tools and Apps for Learning Strategies and Acquiring Skills

Tools and Apps mentioned above:

PearDeck: https://www.peardeck.com/

FlipGrid: https://flipgrid.com/

Wakelet: http://www.wakelet.com/

Book Creator: https://bookcreator.com/

Trello: https://trello.com/

Buncee: https://app.edu.buncee.com/

My eCoach: https://my-ecoach.com

Activity: Research Apps, Learning Strategies, and Skills

Consider what you came up with for your Learner Profile and the skills you already have. Do you notice any gaps? Have you ever wished you had an app or tool that would help you be able to do something better? This is the time to do your research on any apps and tools you want to try.

Now it's your turn to collect different apps and tools for your backpack.

Apps and Tools	Learning Strategies	Skills and Competencies

Personal Learning Backpack

After I compiled different apps, strategies, skills, and competencies, I aligned those with what I came up with for my Learner Profile. I added more apps, tools, conferences, and other resources I might need for my Personal Learning Backpack. Below is an example of specific strategies and resources that I included to guide me so I can learn with a purpose.

	Skills, Dispositions, and Competencies	Learning Strategies	Tools, Apps, Resources
Engagement	Self-confidence, Growth Mindset, Active listening	Watch videos and participate in webinars, podcasts, courses, and conferences to discuss strategies around purpose. Use the power of "Yet" more.	Ted Talks, YouTube, SXSW EDU, ISTE, iNACOL, Zoom, TED Masterclass, My PLN
Representation	Organization, Choice of best resources to support learning	Use multiple formats to read and research. Investigate different tools and strategies for podcasting and collaborating.	YouTube Channel, Anchor, Burberry, WordPress, Wakelet
Action and Expression	Creativity, collaboration, divergent thinking	Organize tasks and to-do lists in collaborative space. Create engaging graphics in interactive presentations.	Trello Board, Padlet, PearDeck, My eCoach, Canva, Buncee

Table. 5.7 My Personal Learning Backpack

What I found out was the first thing I needed to do was to build my self-confidence around finding my purpose. That meant changing my mindset and using the power of YET more. I am not sure what tools I will need to learn, YET. If I say I don't think I can write another book, I need to add YET. If I say, I'm not sure how to do this or that, I need to add YET. Changing my mindset by adding the word YET opens up the possibilities about what my backpack will look like in a year.

I tried this process in several workshops. So far, the feedback was great and helpful. As I said, I am still learning, so I probably will make some changes with what I will need for my future. I am curious to see the backpack YOU create and the conversations YOU have about your learning.

Pause/Think/Reflect
Who knows what the future will hold for us?
How will you become future-ready?
What will you need to develop agency?

Activity: Create Your Personal Learning Backpack

This activity is great to do alone or with someone. I remember creating my backpack and then sharing it with several colleagues. One asked me why I didn't add My eCoach. I was using that already but never thought that could be where I organize my materials and presentations. Having another person to bounce off ideas helped me rethink my learning strategies.

Create your Personal Learning Backpack and fill it out to keep with your journal.

	Skills, Dispositions, and Competencies	Learning Strategies	Tools, Apps, Resources
Engagement			
Representation			
Action & Expression			

 The object of education is to prepare the young to educate themselves throughout their lives."

— LEV VYGOTSKY (1930)

Profiles, Passion Projects, Portfolios

I've known Michael Mohammad, a high school science teacher in Elmbrook School District in Wisconsin, for several years. When you meet Mike, you can tell he is passionate about personalizing learning for all learners. I was fortunate to have a conversation with Mike on my podcast for Episode #25 and to present with him at the ISTE 2019 (International Society for Technology in Education) conference. This is where I learned more about how his students create their learner profiles, design passion projects, and student portfolios. I asked him to share, and I am glad he said yes.

* * *

Profile Driven Learning
by Mike Mohammad

I was born to two immigrant parents from Pakistan who became US citizens. Like many second-generation Americans, my parents wanted my life to be better than their own. In their minds, that meant me becoming a doctor, and this meant a strong focus on science classes in my schooling. In my elementary years, I loved science. But that interest waned in my high school years. I quickly discovered that I didn't have much passion for these classes that were mostly lecture. My interest was drawn to my literature and writing classes in which I was given the freedom to create and explore texts that sparked my interest. It wasn't until I got to college-level science that I finally got the hands-on science experiences my high school experience lacked, and my interest in science was rekindled.

I tell my students that I can't remember anything we did in my high school physics course that was meaningful to my life beyond getting that science credit. I want it to be different for the learners in my classroom. That starts with learning about each student.

- How can we amplify their strengths and reduce the obstacles to learning in our classroom?
- How can we tap into their interests, so what we're doing is relevant to their lives now?
- What are their aspirations so that we can make this class relevant to their future?

These connections cannot be made without taking the time to have learners reflect on their own strengths, challenges, interests, and aspirations. That is where the learner profile comes in. Students may have given a cursory reflection on these ideas, but constructing a document communicating these ideas forces them to define these areas more concretely than many have done before. When students share this information with teachers, it helps educators build experiences that will tap into those interests and aspirations. While they may end up sharing this document with others, the profile is for the learner. It is to help the learner advocate for their own needs and help justify the choices they make in their education.

In our classroom, our first step is to have students begin communicating their interests and aspirations, which becomes the first part of their student portfolio. This portfolio is a student-created Google Site where students house information about themselves as a person and learner, including artifacts and reflections from their classwork. The first step of the portfolio process is creating a page to communicate these interests and aspirations on a Passion Page. Students embed YouTube videos to communicate to others what matters in their lives.

A wonderful way we connect standards to passions is student passion projects. Through these 12-hour projects, students are able to explore a personal interest or curiosity by implementing science practices. They ultimately present their projects to peers and parents at a project expo. Their work for these projects is also housed in their portfolio.

Example Student Portfolios

http://bit.ly/studentportfolio-
mohammad

Email: mohammam@elmbrookschools.org
Website: http://mophysicsmoproblems.blogspot.com/
Twitter: @mo_physics

Episode #25: Building the Why for Learning
https://barbarabray.net/2018/01/05/building-the-why-for-
learning-with-mike-mohammad/

* * *

Questions to Ponder

- Why do we need to continue to learn new skills throughout our lives? What skills will you want to develop?
- What jobs do you believe will be lost, and by when? What new jobs do you think will take their place?
- How does UDL help you discover your WHY for learning?
- How can your Personal Learning Backpack support your learning? How can portfolios help you demonstrate what you learned?

Wonderings

I used to think that we needed to address only our challenges to help us grow. After several years of conversations, focus groups, and accepting my mistakes, I realized that to prepare for our future, we need to focus on our strengths, interests, and aspirations along with understanding that everyone can find strategies and support to help reduce barriers if they know what they are. We need to believe in ourselves and become confident that we can achieve what we aspire to become. All of us have challenges that can overwhelm us. When we are stronger and are okay about being vulnerable, we can share our challenges by addressing and facing them. We may even turn a challenge into one of our strengths. That doesn't happen right away, especially for children who struggle and have trauma in their lives. Every one of us has gifts to share and challenges to overcome. Creating a Learner Profile and Personal Learning Backpack gives us tools, strategies, and resources to realistically take on our strengths and challenges to help us grow and learn on purpose. What we learn, we can share and model for others.

* * *

If you are looking for additional resources and more about this chapter, go to:

- the book study questions, go to https://barbarabray.net
- digital resources, go to http://bit.ly/defineyourwhy-digital
- discussions on Twitter, use the hashtag #defineyourWHY

WHY FIND YOUR IKIGAI?

生き甲斐

" *Only staying active will make you want to live a hundred years.*"

— JAPANESE PROVERB

What is ikigai?

Ikigai is the Japanese concept of "a reason for being." Everyone has an *ikigai.* To find it requires a journey of self-discovery. The search is worth it. Your *ikigai* is the meaning of your life. Some people have found their *ikigai*, while others are still looking for it. They may not be aware that they carry their *ikigai* with them throughout their lives. It's your path to self-realization, unique to you in every way.

Our ikigai is different for all of us, but one thing we have in common is that we are all searching for meaning."

— HECTOR GARCIA PUIGCERVER

There is no word for "retirement" in Japan. The Ohsaki Study (Sone et al., 2008) found that some of the happiest and longest-living people in the world are from Okinawa, Japan. There the average lifespan is seven years longer than in North America. Okinawa has more 100-year-olds than anywhere else in the world. Instead of retirement, the Okinawans have a word called *ikigai* (pronounced like "icky guy"), which roughly translates to "the reason you get out of bed in the morning." It's the thing that drives you the most.

In the Ohsaki Study, the results showed that the risk of all-cause mortality was significantly higher among the subjects who did not find a sense of *ikigai* as compared with those subjects who found a sense of ikigai. (Pasricha, 2016)

In a 2001 research paper on *ikigai*, co-author Akihiro Hasegawa, a clinical psychologist and associate professor at Toyo Eiwa University, placed the word *ikigai* as part of the everyday Japanese language. It is composed of two words: iki, which means life and gai, that describes value or worth.

According to Hasegawa, the origin of the word *ikigai* goes back to the Heian period (794 to 1185). "Gai comes from the word kai ("shell" in Japanese), which was deemed highly valuable, and from there, *ikigai* derived as a word that means value in living." Hasegawa discovered that Japanese people believe that the sum of small joys in everyday life results in a more fulfilling life as a whole (Mitsuhashi, 2017).

 Enjoy the little things in life, for one day you'll look back and realize they were the big things."

— KURT VONNEGUT

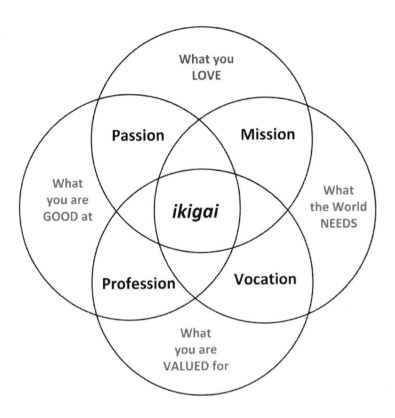

I used to think that making money would lead me to a fulfilled life. That's the reason why I stayed working as a dental hygienist. It was a great job, paid me well, and I was able to work part-time while raising my children. The money was good, but the value was missing for me.

 You can play the game and you can act out the part, even though you know it wasn't written for you."

— JAMES TAYLOR LYRIC

The Four Elements of ikigai

ikigai is similar to passion but holds a strong "purposeful" connotation. The Japanese see the discovery of your *ikigai* as requiring a deep, long search within yourself that can bring about satisfaction and meaning to life. *ikigai* has nothing to do with income. Start with these four primary elements to determine your reason for living:

- What you *Love*
- What you are *Good* at
- What the *World Needs*
- What you are *Valued* for

How do we balance all of these factors in the creation of a life which is meaningful, purposeful, and aligned with our true calling? Is it possible to have it all? The essence of *ikigai* gives you a framework to balance these elements into a cohesive whole. While you can make lists of the four elements above and figure out what it is at the center of them all, finding your *ikigai* can also be as easy as just stopping yourself throughout the day and asking yourself: *"Why am I doing this?"*

When I learned about *ikigai*, I realized I could use it to find what I'm most passionate about. When I started teaching, I changed my thinking about who I was.

What You Love

All of us have things we love, but we may not have written them all in one place. What I love:

my family, learning, gardening, being with friends, connecting to people that push my thinking, playing games like mahjong, watching videos to learn, being with my granddaughter, theater, dancing, writing, reading, listening to podcasts, stories, telling stories, meditating, stretching, walking, photography, classic movies, most genres of music, playing the piano

Now it's your turn. Consider the following bullet points and write in your journal what you love.

- Start thinking about the things that you love using keywords, phrases, and any ideas.
- Brainstorm all the aspects of your life that make your heart sing and even add more later.

What You are Good At

All of us have strengths, skills, and dispositions that make us who we are. I wrote below what people have told me what they believe I'm good at:

Connecting educators and thought leaders, writing, interviewing people during the podcasts, telling stories, actively listening (still working on this one), seeing the big picture, facilitating discussions and meetings, designing graphics, enjoying playing, designing activities for teachers, mediating, endorsing and promoting others, speaking, problem-solving, design thinking

Now it's your turn. Refer back to Chapter 4 and the strengths you came up with about *you*. Consider these questions and answer them in your journal.

- What unique skills do you have that come most naturally to you?
- What dispositions do you believe you have that you will need for your future?
- What talents have you cultivated, and what do you excel at even when you aren't trying?

What the World Needs

I've always wanted to make a difference. Some of the things I've done and still want to do:

I want to help teachers build relationships with their students that start with empathy and grow with compassion and kindness. I am a TeachSDGs ambassador and want to share the UN Global Goals with teachers, so they connect their classrooms globally. I believe young people will be the ones that make the difference since it is their future. I am Agent WHY for #Agents4Agency, so I collaborate with others to develop ways to empower young people (Gen Z) to develop agency.

There is so much happening in the world that to keep on going, you may tune some or most of it out. But the world needs you. It could be in a large way working on a cause you believe in. Or it could be an idea or something you've always wanted to do to change the world in even a small way. Think about these questions as you brainstorm ideas in your journal.

- What breaks your heart or pulls at your gut?
- What change would you most love to create in the world?
- What would you give your life for?

What You are Valued For

I changed this element from "What You Can Get Paid For" to "What You Are Valued For" because value isn't always about money. At this time in my life, I've been rethinking where I am appreciated and feel valued.

I can do keynotes, activities, and workshops around Define Your WHY. I'm planning on creating several short courses, do a book study, and create some videos. I'm hoping people like my book, buy it, share it, and recommend it. I still love coaching and working with teachers and leaders on-site and online. I have several more books I've been wanting to write.

You may have a job now, are looking for a job, or trying to figure out other ways to bring in extra money. You may be an entrepreneur or an Edupreneur and have ideas that you would like to pursue. You may be in a job that is not working for you or would like to volunteer for a cause you believe in. Consider the following questions about your value or what you can get paid for or how others can appreciate you. Share your ideas in your journal.

- What service, value, or offering do you bring or could bring that brings real value to others?
- What is something people need and are happy to pay for or share some value in exchange?

> *Follow your heart and your intuition. They somehow already know what you truly want to become."*
>
> — STEVE JOBS

Discovering your *ikigai* can be one of the greatest journeys you can embark on. However, it can be challenging with many ups and downs. Just remember, it does not happen overnight. As Diana Ross once said, "you can't sit there and wait for people to give you that golden dream; you've got to get out there and make it happen for yourself" (Gill, 2017).

Activity: Combine ikigai Elements

Each element combines with another element in *ikigai*. To discover your *ikigai*, you must first find what you're most passionate about. Then, you can explore the medium through which you can express that passion. Review what you wrote for each of the two elements and write a reflection summarizing how they connect for you.

What You Love + What You're Good At ----> PASSION
What You Love + What the World Needs ----> MISSION
What the World Needs + What You are Valued For ----> VOCATION
What You Are Good At + What You are Valued For ---->
PROFESSION

| Fig. 6.2 *ikigai* going deeper

Activity: Going even deeper to find your ikigai

Where the elements intersect, you can expand on the last activity. For the first intersection (Passion + Mission), consider what you are passionate about and what the world needs? Coming up with ideas for the areas that intersect might take some time, but come back and rethink each of these and write what you came up with in your journal.

1. Passion + Mission	How can you align your passion with your mission about what you love and what you are good at? Is there a cause you believe in that you are passionate about?
2. Mission + Vocation	How does your mission about what you love align to what the world needs and what you can be valued for?
3. Passion + Profession	How are you valued about what you are good at and love to do? What can you do to bring more value around your passion?
4. Vocation + Profession	How have you focused on what you are good at with what you are doing now? What could you do that brings you more value and appreciation? What could you get paid for?

Connecting ikigai with Conversations about the WHY

I connected with Shelly Vohra @raspberryberet3 on Twitter when I was trying to figure out my WHY years ago. We have the greatest long-distance conversations (I'm in California and Shelly is in Toronto, Canada) about our journeys and what we wanted to do next. I had just learned about *ikigai* and shared that with her. We talked about our WHY with transforming education, what we could do to make teachers feel more valued, and so on. She was working on her doctorate, and I had just started my podcast. I loved our conversations and just had to have a conversation with her on my podcast that I was just starting. I invited Shelly to be on Episode #3, and we talked about her journey into inquiry. We both were asking lots of questions and seeking our WHY. Right after her podcast, we decided to start the #rethink_learning chat. That was over three years ago, and we love every chat and the discussions on Twitter. We are rethinking our *ikigai* each time we talk. I asked Shelly if she would share her WHY that she is writing about for her upcoming book.

To Share My Story So Others Share Theirs
By Shelly Vohra

I grew up during a time when there were not a lot of racialized students in my school or in my neighborhood. I was one of a handful of minority students from Asia in my K-12 school. In my class, there was only one other East Indian girl and no African-Canadian or other Asian students (e.g., East Asian, Southeast Asians). I remember in Grade 8, I went to India for my cousin's wedding in November and missed about a month of school. My Geography teacher wanted me to do a presentation about India and the wedding upon my return, and I was excited to do so because I felt it was important to educate my classmates about my culture, traditions, and values.

Although my classmates thought the bride's clothing, jewelry, and makeup were "cool," I felt they truly did not understand my perspectives or my experiences. Looking back now, I do not completely blame them. I grew up in a time when there were not a lot of minority students in the educational system, but I still feel that should not have been a reason or excuse for teachers not to integrate issues related to diversity, equity, inclusion, and social justice in the classroom.

In my language class, I wasn't very engaged because I never saw myself represented in any of the materials we read (e.g., novels, short stories, poetry), but I went through the motions, worked hard, and earned good grades. I felt the same way in my science, math, and history classes; all we ever talked about were contributions of white people in these disciplines when there was ample evidence that Asians and Africans made significant contributions in these areas. It was frustrating for me, and when I spoke up about it, I felt I was ignored, patronized, or being told I was being 'confrontational.'

When I became an educator, I promised myself I would integrate issues related to social justice and equity in my classroom with my students. Initially, I found it challenging for a variety of reasons; there were not enough resources, not a lot of novels and books that represented my students' experiences or culture, and not a lot of support from certain stakeholders. However, I forged ahead and did the best I could with what I had. My students and I had conversations and conducted research on racism, discrimination, and privilege. We brainstormed ideas in ways that we could educate others. We felt it was important to have these conversations to deepen understanding about these issues and hopefully contribute in a small way to make this world a better place. I found, due to my own racialized identity, my students could relate to me in ways they could not relate to their other teachers. They were so happy when they found out I was East Indian, and they could talk to me about Bollywood movies, Diwali, their favorite foods, and their trips back home. Their faces would light up when I wore a salwar kameez to school during Asian Heritage Month in May and when I told them they could talk to me in Hindi, Punjabi, or Urdu. This not only made them feel valued, but they felt they were being represented in the school body because one of their teachers was from the same background as them and their families.

Then, in 2005, I completely changed how I taught. I still integrated issues related to equity, inclusion, and social justice, but I centered these concepts around a big idea and driving question, which integrated curriculum expectations from a variety of disciplines.

This is my WHY—to share my experiences and ensure our students feel represented, valued, and know someone cares about their stories, experiences, traditions, and values.

Twitter Handle: @raspberryberet3
Website: https://techdiva29.wordpress.com
Episode #3 Podcast and Post: My Journey into Inquiry https://barbarabray.net/2017/06/23/my-journey-into-inquiry/

* * *

Purpose is the reason you journey. Passion is the fire that lights your way."

— AUTHOR UNKNOWN

Questions to Ponder

- In working on *ikigai*, have you found out something about yourself that surprised you?
- How can *ikigai* help you build your self-confidence and encourage self-advocacy?
- What did you find as your passion?
- Is there something you have always wanted to do to make a difference?

Wonderings

When I first learned about *ikigai*, I really wanted to learn as much as I could. I couldn't believe that something that simple was there and I didn't know about it. I watched videos, read different books, and did additional research on *ikigai*. I started sharing what I found out about *ikigai* at conferences and was amazed that very few people in the western world had ever heard about it. Actually, I didn't really know that much about *ikigai* until I started doing more research on it in 2015. I am not surprised that people in the U.S. didn't know about it. I wanted to share it far and wide. I wrote about it. Talked about it. I received great feedback from people who were also trying to figure out their WHY.

I hope that when you read this chapter, you come back to it and rethink your *ikigai* at different times in your life, just like I did.

* * *

If you are looking for additional resources and more about this chapter, go to:

- the book study questions, go to https://barbarabray.net
- digital resources, go to http://bit.ly/defineyourwhy-digital
- discussions on Twitter, use the hashtag #defineyourWHY

WHY HAVE EMPATHY FOR YOU?

> *I think we all have empathy. We may not have enough courage to display it."*
>
> — MAYA ANGELOU

All of us have stress in our lives. We are living in an uncertain world that impacts how we handle what we do and how we react to stress. This chapter starts with why we need empathy for ourselves. I read Brené Brown's book *Daring Greatly: How the Courage to Be Vulnerable Transforms the Way We Live, Love, Parent, and Lead* and have been following her for years. What I've learned is that it takes courage to be the authentic you.

> *If we can share our story with someone who responds with empathy and understanding, shame can't survive."*
>
> — BRENÉ BROWN

Video on empathy:
https://youtu.be/1Evwgu369Jw

This video on empathy helped me understand what it means to care about others. Empathy is feeling with people. Take a moment to view and then reflect in your journal on what you learned from the video linked here.

Fear of Failure

I decided to step out of my comfort zone. I wanted to try some new experiences, but something was holding me back. I couldn't figure it out. I think what was keeping me from finding my WHY was fear. Fear of not having enough money, so I kept taking jobs that kept me doing what I thought was comfortable. Fear of looking foolish, so I kept doing the same presentations the same way. Fear of letting my family down. Actually, my family was pushing me to go out of my comfort zone. I didn't realize I had a fixed mindset thinking that I couldn't do something new or different. This type of thinking was me holding me back. I realized I was making excuses to stay in my comfort zone. To define my WHY, I had to grow and learn and change. So I decided to start over and rethink what I was doing with my life. I needed to explore my WHY, my purpose. I tried to figure out why I was letting fear take over me. I reached out for help from my family, friends, therapist, and coach. I found that I had to know my fears if I wanted to overcome them.

Some teachers have told me they were afraid they would be found out. I dug deeper. It was that crazy "Impostor Syndrome" they were talking about. Traditionally teachers are supposed to be the expert in the room. Many have told me that they fake knowing everything. Oh my! I've been there. It is the experience of feeling like a phony—you feel as though at any moment, you are going to be found out as a fraud. Since I felt like this and was a coach for others who shared this same feeling, I needed to stop feeling like an impostor by not thinking like one. If this sounds like you, read the 10 Steps to Overcome the Impostor Syndrome. https://impostorsyndrome.com/10-steps-overcome-impostor/

 F.E.A.R. *can have several meanings like these two:*

Forget Everything And Run

OR

Face Everything And Rise

The choice is yours."

— Zig Ziglar

Fear can be a good thing. It keeps you safe and encourages you to be cautious when there are times that you need to be. But fear can also limit you. Not everything you're afraid of deserves for you to be afraid or cautious. Sometimes, courage and bravery are needed to make your life better. First, review your fears and see if they are real.

False
Evidence
Appearing
Real

I had no idea I was holding myself back when I didn't have to. So I took the time to address each fear one at a time and talk about that fear. I needed to figure out on a scale of one to ten how real the fears really were.

A few of my Fears that I rated from 1 to 10 (10 as the scariest fear for me):

- Saying NO instead of YES 4
- Saying YES instead of NO 5
- Changing my direction 6
- Feeling like an impostor.........6
- Looking foolish.......................5
- Not having enough money......7
- Letting my family down.........8

There were no fears in my life that were 10s. I made the fears bigger than they really were. Actually jumping out of a plane is high on the list, but one day, I'll take that on.

Activity: Knowing your Fears

All of us have fears that we may make bigger than they really are. I have talked to some people who told me they will never fly because they know the plane they are on will crash. Others have told me they were afraid to travel alone. The list goes on. What about yours? How about rating your fears?

In your journal, list your fears and rate them from 1-10 (with 10 the scariest).

- not having enough money
- letting myself down
- not having enough energy
-

After I identified and rated some of my fears, I needed to do research on different topics. I needed to reinvent myself. That seemed so big that I just kept doing the same thing, even though it wasn't working for me. I guess I didn't feel confident in myself. I needed to get out and talk to people, visit schools, and travel. This is a mental trick anyone needs to do. It is about believing that you can do something if you do the research on what it is you want to do. The research builds knowledge. When you have that knowledge, you can build the confidence you need to move forward.

Pause/Think/Reflect

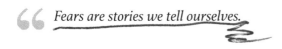 *Fears are stories we tell ourselves.*

— LAURA DAVIS

Stress and Burnout

All of us have stress in our lives. We are living in an uncertain world. Stress can be perceived as negative if we don't know how to react to that stress. There are signs that the stress you believe you cannot handle may be leading you toward burnout.

Stress is when you have too many pressures that demand too much of you physically and psychologically. When you are stressed, you may still imagine that if you can just get everything under control, you will feel better. Stress involves "too much."

Being burned out means feeling empty, without any motivation, and beyond caring about what happens to you. When you experience burnout, you often don't see any hope of positive change in your situations. Burnout means "not enough" or cannot cope anymore.

Excessive stress is like drowning in responsibilities. Burnout is like being all dried up.

Stress	Burnout
Characterized by overengagement	Characterized by disengagement
Emotions are overreactive	Emotions are blunted
Produces urgency and hyperactivity	Produces helplessness and hopelessness
Loss of energy	Loss of motivation, ideals, and hope
Leads to anxiety disorders	Leads to detachment and depression
Primary damage is physical	Primary damage is emotional

(Serveyev, 2019)

Table 7.1 Stress vs. Burnout

A study on Teacher Burnout found stress and burnout to be the top threat to workplace health, resulting in losses in job satisfaction, retention, culture, and revenue. Teacher burnout is on the rise.

"Compared to 10 years ago, the evidence I have is that there are much more stress and demands on teachers in the U.S.," wrote Jon Snyder, Stanford researcher (Snyder, 2016) and explained that we need to explore schedules and time teachers in different countries spend in direct contact with students. Dion Burns, one of Snyder's colleagues at SCOPE and a senior researcher at the Learning Policy Institute (https://learningpolicyinstitute.org/), wrote that the things that keep teachers in the profession are *"working conditions that include the support from leadership, opportunities for collaboration and decision-making within the school, and access to resources for teaching and learning."*

 To be yourself in a world that is constantly trying to make you something else is the greatest accomplishment."

— RALPH WALDO EMERSON

Empathy is about caring for others, but it also means caring for YOU. Educators and other professionals in the service industry who serve others tend to not take care of themselves first. It is not selfish to take care of you, but many of us went into education to be there for kids first. Because of the demands of the profession and many other issues, educators can become easily overwhelmed and find that they cannot handle stress or issues in their lives.

Overcoming Stress

Mandy Froehlich's book, *The Fire Within*, includes stories about depression and stress, and how to take care of yourself. When I first read her book, I was pulled into how she shared her fears and was being vulnerable. It touched me. I was lucky to have a conversation in Episode #79 with her about what she learned about herself during the writing process. I've learned from Mandy, who is also my coach through the publishing process for EduMatch Publishing, and honored that she included her WHY on self-care.

* * *

Self-Care
By Mandy Froehlich

I remember the first time I flew in a plane and listened to the flight attendant say, "Put your mask on first before helping others." My mind immediately went to the worst-case scenario: trouble on the plane, masks drop, oxygen is low, and I look at my son gasping, and I'm supposed to do what? Put my own mask on first? Had they lost their minds? What kind of mother would I be if the first thing I did was put my mask on before my child?

Similarly, as a teacher, I had been told that the students come first. Like a parent, we put our own needs aside to focus on them. If we get tired, others say, "Join the club." If we need a day off, we wait by the computer, hoping to find a sub until it gets approved. If we need to go to the bathroom, well, we just don't. The kind of people who go into the teaching profession are generally selfless and empathetic to others. Taking care of ourselves when there's never enough time in the day to get everything done feels like we are taking away from someone else, which deviates from why we began teaching to begin with. Self-care feels counterintuitive.

However, there are side-effects to ignoring your own needs. Burnout is common in the education profession. Symptoms include ailments like high blood pressure or a weakened immune system, becoming increasingly cynical, irritable and angry, and fatigue. In a profession where there is so much riding on our effectiveness, it's difficult to avoid burnout entirely, but one of the ways to fight against it is by practicing self-care. Self-care allows you to remember what it's like to feel *like you*. And while some people would say that one needs to practice balance, I would argue that self-care helps you feel balanced. Our busy lives ebb and flow. Sometimes we may work more when things are busy, and sometimes, we need more family time. Understanding that the time we spend on personal and professional time will rarely be equal is also a form of self-care.

The idea of putting our masks on first is important because if we are not at our best, there is no chance we are giving our best. There are many amazing differences that we can make as long as we have enough to give, and it's impossible to do that without practicing self-care and feeling balanced. When we are not whole, it leaves the loved ones around us to fend for themselves without our assistance to guide them properly. Our students deserve to have us at our peak, and we deserve to be happy and healthy people, and that is why putting your mask on first before you save the rest of the world is the right move.

Twitter: @froehlichm
Website: https://mandyfroehlich.com/
Email: mandyfroehlichedu@gmail.com
Author: The Fire Within http://bit.ly/firewithinbook (Froehlich, M. 2018)
Author: Divergent EDU http://bit.ly/divergent_edu

Episode #79 Podcast: Leadership, Innovation, and Divergent Teaching http://bit.ly/episode79-froehlich

* * *

Mind FULL or Mindful

When we are born, our minds are empty and open to learning. Through the years, we collect experiences, opinions, ideas, problems we want to solve, concerns about others and ourselves, and much more. Our minds tend to be too full of things like to-do lists, recent discussions, tests, thoughts, and distractions, to name a few. The mind loves to keep busy. It is tough for us to tame all that inner chatter going on in our heads. When your mind is full, it is difficult to listen to others because our mind is somewhere else. Somewhere along our journey, we may reach a breaking point as if our brain is on overload and our mind is too FULL.

Mind FULL for me is when I keep adding two more things on my to-do list for each item I check off. This is when I know I am too busy to take in each moment.

Check out my post about this quote: https://barbarabray.net/2016/01/12/being-or-doing/

I was becoming a "Human DOING," not a "Human BEING."

Consider these questions as you read more about any stress you may be experiencing.

- *Are you experiencing more anxiety and stress than ever before?*
- *How can you lessen the day-to-day stress you feel and*
- *bring more clarity, calmness, and joy into your life?*

Mindfulness is the ability for us to wake up, pay attention, and be more intentional about getting the most out of our lives. Being mindful is the ability to be fully present, aware of where we are and what we're doing, and not be overly reactive or overwhelmed by what's going on around us.

 Mindfulness is awareness that arises through paying attention, on purpose, in the present moment, non-judgmentally, And then I sometimes add, in the service of self-understanding and wisdom."

— Jon Kabat-Zinn

Jon Kabat-Zinn details in his YouTube video the "9 Attitudes of Mindfulness." When I listened to his explanations about each of these attitudes, I realized I needed to review these and practice them one at a time over and over. To be the best YOU and know your WHY, being mindful and understanding where you are with these attitudes can help you get to know YOU better.

Watch and Reflect on "9 Attitudes of Mindfulness"
https://youtu.be/2n7FOBFMvXg

Here are the times for each of the attitudes in Kabat-Zinn's video.

1. (2:37) Beginner's Mind
2. (5:04) Non-Judging
3. (9:00) Acceptance
4. (11:55) Letting Go
5. (15:20) Trust
6. (18:20) Patience
7. (20:13) Non-Striving
8. (22:41) Gratitude
9. (23:24) Generosity

awesome

Activity: Mindfulness Attitudes

Mindfulness practice is related to stress reduction by providing the ability to free your mind to be able to deal with unanticipated obstacles and setbacks. Listen to Kabat-Zinn's video and then choose and reflect on one of the attitudes that resonate with you in your journal. Share with a friend how you addressed that attitude, practiced it, and your feelings before and after.

 Mindfulness isn't difficult, we just need to remember to do it."

— SHARON SALZBERG, MINDFULNESS TEACHER

Activity: Mindfulness of Breathing

Trying to calm our minds when too many things are going through it is tough. Have you ever walked into a room to get something and didn't know why you are there? Because our lives are complex, we may be on autopilot doing what we do without even thinking about it. We may be hurrying from task to task going through our to-do lists checking off one at a time. When we are mindful of our breathing and being alive, we can stop, wake up, and enjoy the moment.

Consider an infant curiously discovering her hand. She is totally absorbed in exploring this extension of her body, wondering what it is. She is breathing and taking in everything around her. How can we tap into that complete attention to self and curiosity?

Focus on Your Breathing

You breathe because you are alive, but you probably don't stop and think about what it feels like. You can do this during a break or any time during the day where you can sit quietly.

1. Sit in a comfortable chair with your feet on the floor and back straight away from the back of the chair.
2. Place one hand right above your navel.
3. Breathe in and out normally and focus on the changing physical sensations as your abdomen expands and deflates. Do this for at least one minute.
4. Repeat #3 with counting when you breathe in and now go longer and slower when you breathe out for another minute.
5. Breathe in as deep as you can feel your belly fill up with air and even more slowly and longer let the air out, but this time making a noise deep in your belly. Feel the vibration in your abdomen. Repeat this deep breathing five times.
6. Now put your hands on your knees and breathe like you

normally breathe without counting for about 2-5 minutes. Try to calm your mind while focusing on your breathing.

See if you can focus on your breathing without having your mind wander. Each time you do this breathing activity, calm your mind, and try to focus on feeling the cool air come in and go out warmer. Take time each day for seven days to do this breathing activity and then work up to 10 minutes each day.

Feeling Stressed? Blow on your Thumb

It sounds strange, but blowing on your thumb is a great stress reliever. It works by cooling off the thumb and calming the pulse in it. This, in turn, causes your body to feel more relaxed in general.

 If we practice mindfulness, we always have a place to be when we are afraid."

— THICH NHAT HANH

Living with Uncertainty

Being uncomfortable is kind of the new norm today. The world is changing so quickly that no one knows what is ahead for us. There is uncertainty about the type of work needed in the future. That impacts all of us. For me, I knew I couldn't keep going down the same road because it wasn't working for me. The best habit for me was to practice becoming familiar with uncertainty and being okay to be uncomfortable.

I try to pick one thing each day that kind of scares me and act on it. The one big thing I did was start my podcast show. Each show puts me out of my comfort zone. I needed to push myself, and I did it big time. Now I look forward to each conversation. I really recommend the idea of picking one thing each day that scares you and go and do it. You will be surprised at how you handled scary moments. You will be amazed at how you will be able to live out of your comfort zone and with uncertainty a little more each and every day.

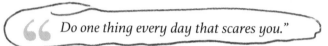

Do one thing every day that scares you."

— Eleanor Roosevelt

Activity: Do one thing that scares you today.

What is that thing that you will take on today? It doesn't have to be big. What if you consider one thing that's new and out of your comfort zone? Be brave today and choose one thing you have been putting off doing either out of fear or just thinking you cannot do it. But you can.

Reflect/Journal
Go ahead and do that one thing today.
Then write what you did in your journal, what happened, and how you felt taking on this fear.

Being Vulnerable

Vulnerability is the act of allowing yourself to expose your thoughts and fears and wishes and dreams, knowing that others might judge and criticize you for doing so. Being vulnerable with yourself is about connecting with your fears and scarier things that are going on inside you.

When I think of vulnerability, I think of Brené Brown and how much I've learned from her books, videos, interviews, and more. Her book *Daring to Lead* and her Netflix special, *Daring Greatly*, opened the door to ideas about being okay about taking risks and being vulnerable. This quote helped me refine my idea of owning our story.

> Owning our story can be hard but not nearly as difficult as spending our lives running from it. Embracing our vulnerabilities is risky but not nearly as dangerous as giving up on love and belonging and joy—the experiences that make us the most vulnerable. Only when we are brave enough to explore the darkness will we discover the infinite power of our light."

— BRENÉ BROWN

I talked with Paul Emerich France about personalized learning and found out much more about Paul and his journey in Episode #78 podcast. He brought up Brené Brown, who I followed, and then we delved deeper into what it means to be vulnerable and taking risks. I was lucky to review his book, *Reclaiming Personalized Learning*, and I just had to ask Paul to write his story he shared with me.

* * *

Being Vulnerable and Sharing Mistakes
By Paul Emerich France

In my third year of teaching, I had begun to explore iPads in the classroom. One day, in particular, I tried to introduce simple machines to my students through a series of exploratory centers. For each center, they would access part of my classroom website, watching videos and reading directions for how to interact with the simple machines at each station.

In my head, it seemed like a great idea. But in practice, it turned out to be utter chaos. The students who weren't off-task seemed confused, resulting in innumerable fires I had to extinguish. If matters couldn't get worse, I heard the handle on my door click, and out of the corner of my eye, I saw the door slowly open. My principal was walking in for an unannounced observation. I began to panic. My palms began to sweat, and I could feel my body temperature start to rise.

"It's bombing!" I said as she walked in, throwing my hands up in the air while chaos continued to consume my classroom.

A smirk crept across her face. She stopped where she was, and kindly said, "Oh, not a problem! Let's find a time to chat about it later!"

She held true to that promise, and not too long after the lesson, she and I sat down to talk about what my intentions were with the lesson, and where it went wrong. Together, we identified the strengths of the plans and the challenges of its implementation, helping me realize a few things. First, I had not scaffolded my students' autonomy with a task like that. I hadn't taught them how to interact with the centers before asking them to engage in this lesson format. Second, some of the technological aspects of the lesson created unnecessary complexity. In this instance, the iPads weren't as necessary as I thought they were. I was using technology simply for the sake of technology.

Instead of feeling ashamed, I left this meeting feeling empowered. I left the conversation with a better understanding of what works--and what doesn't work--in the classroom. And this was because the relationship my former principal and I had allowed for instructional experimentation; it allowed me to be vulnerable and share my mistakes, missteps, and misconceptions, all for the purpose of professional learning.

Website: https://paulemerich.com
Twitter: @paul_emerich
Instagram: @paul_emerich

Emerich France, P. (2019) Reclaiming Personalized Learning. Thousand Oaks, CA: Corwin.

Episode #78 Podcast: Reclaiming Personalized Learning (http://bit. ly/episode78-emerich)

The Concept of Empathy

 Everyone you meet is fighting a battle you know nothing about. Be kind. Always."

— Robin Williams

Empathy: The Human Connection to Patient Care

Human Connection video:
https://youtu.be/cDDWvj_q-o8

This video is about being more than just healing—it builds a connection that encompasses mind, body, and soul. Watch the video and reflect on how it demonstrates what empathy means about understanding everyone has something going on in their lives.

Psychologists Daniel Goleman and Paul Ekman break down the concept of empathy into the following three categories.

Cognitive empathy is the ability to understand how a person feels and what they might be thinking. This means we are better communicators because we can relay information in a way that best reaches the other person.

Emotional empathy is the ability to share the feelings of another person. This type of empathy helps you build emotional connections with others. Some have described it as "your pain in my heart."

Compassionate empathy is about moving us to take action and going beyond simply understanding others and sharing their feelings. It is about helping others however we can.

These three categories of empathy made sense, but to actually use these abilities was another thing. In Design Thinking, empathy is, as explained in IDEO's Human-Centred Design Toolkit (https://www. ideo.com/post/design-kit), a "deep understanding of the problems and realities of the people you are designing for." It involves learning about the difficulties people face, as well as uncovering their latent needs and desires in order to explain their behaviors. To do so, we need to have an understanding of the people's environment, as well as their roles in and interactions with their environment.

Neuroscientists have recently discovered that empathy is hard-wired into the way humans are made and is an integral part of our physiology. They discovered that while humans observe others performing certain actions or experience certain states, the observer's brain activity resembles someone actually engaged in the activity being observed. In other words, empathy is an innate quality that we can all make use of in order to design for the people around us.

 Compassion is not religious business, it is human business, it is not luxury, it is essential for our own peace and mental stability, it is essential for human survival."

— Dalai Lama

I met Dr. Winston Sakurai when he was principal of the lower boys school at St. Andrews School in Honolulu, Hawaii. When I learned about the fourth-grade design thinking studio, I wanted to learn more. I asked him if he could share why empathy matters as part of the design thinking process. Winston is now Director and Principal of Kaohao School in Kailua, Hawaii.

* * *

Empathy in Solving Real-World Problems
By Winston Sakurai

Educators must have a keen understanding of individuals and make a personal investment in working to help them to be successful. In short, they must care for others. When there is a need, time must be spent to understand the situation, reflect upon how best to support, then make wise decisions that benefit both the school and the individual. Schools need to establish authentic opportunities for students to empathize with others. This will only enhance the school culture when it is woven into the fabric of everyone's thoughts and actions.

Students utilize the Design Thinking process, which calls for empathy in solving real-world problems, an idea taken from the Stanford University d.school. Students work in teams to try to understand how to provide the best solution to complicated issues by being aware of the human element that needs to be satisfied. This means inquisitive investigation, observation, data analysis, and reflection on how best to help others. Students then proceed to ideate, design, fabricate, prototype, and test solutions for their "clients" that they are assisting. However, it is empathy that is the first step in the process. Without a good understanding of how to help, what emotions are at play, and looking from another person's point of view, a solution might not actually solve a problem, or even worse might actually cause even bigger issues.

The most fascinating part of seeing our students grow through this protocol is how they grapple with making good decisions when each of them has differing opinions on how to solve a problem. It is that interpersonal dynamic; learning how to read each other, letting go of one's egos, being aware of their vocal tone, showing patience when dealing with frustration that are key learning points that can't be taught through lecture because it has to be experienced. The reflection on the process they went through can be more important than the product outcome. Students now have the foundation to transfer the knowledge of previous team experiences to help lead future group tasks and be more self-aware of their own emotions as they go through the process.

Website: http://winstonsakurai.weebly.com
Twitter: @winstonsakurai Twitter chat: #PrinLeaderchat
Facebook: https://www.facebook.com/pg/winstonsakurai
LinkedIn: https://www.linkedin.com/in/winstonsakurai

Book: *Education Write Now: Top Strategies for Improving Relationships and Culture with multiple authors*
Episode #65: *Lead with Empathy, Design for Innovation*
http://bit.ly/episode65-sakurai

* * *

The Design Thinking Process Starts with Empathy

I used the design thinking process for project-based learning, designing products, and solving problems. I never thought about having empathy for myself until I did a workshop on design thinking and mentioned defining our WHY. One of the teachers brought up using this process to help find our own WHY. It works. The design thinking process starts with empathy.

| Fig. 7.1 Design Thinking Process

Activity: Use the Design Thinking Process about YOU

You can be the best YOU you want to create. Take out your journal and answer the questions using the design thinking process. Start with Empathy for you as the audience you are learning about.

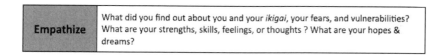

Think of you from a different point-of-view (POV) than you normally look at you. Look at you as if you are on the outside looking in. Consider writing about anything that could be a barrier to keeping you from your WHY.

Define	Look at you from a different perspective about something you are passionate about or believe. What did you find out about you that is a barrier or problem keeping you from finding your purpose?

Brainstorm what lights your fire, what you came up with using *ikigai* and the Golden Circle. Add notes on how you can address what is keeping you from finding your WHY.

Ideate	Brainstorm ideas of what could be the passion that lights your fire and defines your purpose How can you address what is keeping you from finding or pursuing your WHY? Cluster similar ideas. Passion + Beliefs + Ways to Pursue Purpose

A prototype can be an idea, especially when you are talking about you and your WHY. You can take that idea and create it in a form that you feel comfortable sharing with others.

Prototype	Create a prototype of how you plan to develop a passion that can define your purpose; your WHY. The prototype can be an idea in the form of a journal, drawing, podcast, video, a personal beliefs statement. or other form.

When you share your ideas, you are open to change and ideas from others. It is up to you, but your network can be there for you.

Test	Share your prototype with others for feedback. Go ahead and take a chance and share it on social media. Reflect on the feedback you receive, and then revise if needed and share again.

Share your prototype with others for feedback. Go ahead and take a chance and share it on social media. Reflect on the feedback you receive, and then revise if needed and share again.

 I've finally stopped running away from myself. Who else is there better to be?

— GOLDIE HAWN

Questions to Ponder

- How do you develop empathy for yourself instead of focusing on problems that keep you from moving forward?
- How do you handle and manage stress?

- What fears do you have that you want to overcome?
- What do you do for self-care?

Wonderings

I have seen and experienced situations where people I know and cared for kept moving down a path that was not good for them. I realized through my own experiences that I could not change the path they chose. Nothing I said would help, but I could model by moving through tough choices that I made. It is all about the choices we make; some good, some bad. It's how we handle those choices. I've made many wrong choices and some because I thought I had to be "right." When I did the work to have empathy for me and look at me from different perspectives, I realized that being "right" or thinking I had to be "perfect" was all in my head. That's called an "Inside Job" because we make excuses for ourselves or focus on other people instead of taking care of us first. I'm now trying to use pause more, look at what I'm doing from a different perspective, before I make a quick decision or react too fast.

 Remember to look up at the stars and not down at your feet. Try to make sense of what you see and wonder about what makes the universe exist.

BE CURIOUS!

And however difficult life may seem, there is always something you can do and succeed at. It matters that you don't just give up."

— STEPHEN HAWKING

* * *

If you are looking for additional resources and more about this chapter, go to:

- the book study questions, go to https://barbarabray.net
- digital resources, go to http://bit.ly/defineyourwhy-digital
- discussions on Twitter, use the hashtag #defineyourWHY

WHY DISCOVER YOUR PASSIONS AND WHAT YOU LOVE?

> *Your visions will become clear only when you can look into your own heart. Who looks outside, dreams; who looks inside, awakes."*

— C.G. JUNG

Take What You Love Deeper

Several years ago, I watched Steve Jobs's commencement speech on YouTube that he gave to the Stanford graduates in 2005. It was a tear-jerker. He mentioned to the graduates to do what you are passionate about and added, "do what makes your heart sing." I love that. He also shared that he had cancer and that each day, each moment, each breath matters because you never know when it is

Steve Jobs speech:
youtu.be/UF8uR6Z6KLc

your last. I was touched by his speech. I thought about what he said and the idea of making your heart sing for a long time.

If You Haven't Found It Yet, Keep Looking.

— STEVE JOBS

I realized I really didn't know what made my heart sing. Mainly I was confused because I had too much I loved to do. I knew that I loved spending time with my family, being with good friends, reading, gardening, discovering new ideas, working with teachers, sharing the stories about innovative strategies and kids making a difference, transforming teaching and learning, playing games, writing, dancing, and writing some more. My list kept growing. I wanted to make a difference and have a balance in my life. That's good. Right? But what do I focus on?

Consider Reading

Find Your Element by Sir Ken Robinson (Robinson, 2014) helped me learn about my passion through a mind map and a vision board.

I was really out of balance. I was working all the time and, to this day, still tend to work way too much. I know I've heard about doing what you love and how that will make you happy. I thought I was doing that. Yet, I had too much on my plate, too much I wanted to do that it was way out of control. I always think of this quote from Confucius and decided to reflect on it with you.

If you love what you do, you will never work a day in your life."

— CONFUCIUS

Does this quote mean that you find something you love and make that your career? That's what I thought I was doing. Most teachers go into teaching because they want to make a difference. If you are a teacher reading this, I'm sure you went into the profession for the kids, not the money. But I've heard from many educators how stressed they are, how hard they work, how they feel unappreciated, and the worst is how they cannot live on their salary. I know teachers who pay for all their own supplies, have one or two other jobs to pay their bills, and some are considering leaving teaching. Many have told me that they do not feel appreciated and valued. The list goes on too long when teaching should be the most valuable and important profession. I mean, after all, they are teaching our future.

No matter what profession you are in, do you feel appreciated and valued? Maybe you're not working or have retired. Do you feel appreciated and valued? Are you a student or parent? Do you feel appreciated and valued? I know it seems like I'm repeating myself here, but I'm trying to make a point. Let's get back to that thing that keeps you up at night. It may be something completely different than your profession.

 Wonder is the beginning of wisdom."

— Socrates

Wonder and Gratitude

When we're young, we have a sense of wonder. Everything is new and exciting. I've heard this quote, *"the world is your oyster."* I'm assuming that means that you can do anything if you put your mind to it. The world is there waiting for you. But it seems a little tougher and more expensive to live now. So what can we do if times are tough? I say it's time to bring the wonder back. You see, attitude is everything. When times are tough, and you don't feel appreciated or valued, that's when you need *An Attitude of Gratitude*. When I feel down, I take out my gratitude jar and write something I wonder about or am grateful for. I found that you can't be depressed and be grateful at the same time.

Try it! If you can't find something to be grateful for at the time, then write down something you wonder about. Push your thinking to wonder and find something you are curious about. Write it down!

| Fig. 8.1 Gratitude Jar

When I'm really down, I go to my Gratitude Jar and pick out a slip of paper to read. There's always something I wrote that makes me smile.

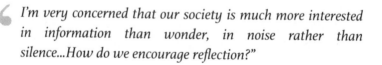

I'm very concerned that our society is much more interested in information than wonder, in noise rather than silence...How do we encourage reflection?"

— MISTER ROGERS

What Drives Wonder

Curiosity drives the wonder. I met Dr. Lindsay Portnoy at a Play Conference, where she did the keynote on how curiosity can look like play. We had been talking via social media for months and had the best time playing together. We ended up going to the SXSW EDU 2018 conference together and doing a lot of giggling. After getting to know Lindsay and reading her articles, I realized I was in the presence of an artist. She knows how to put research, ideas, and words together that go deeper and make sense for any reader. I asked Lindsay to share some research on curiosity and why it matters to wonder, play, and to push our thinking. I'm honored that she agreed.

* * *

Curiosity and Play
By Dr. Lindsay Portnoy

Did you know that infants fall an average of 17 times per hour when learning how to walk? In a study at the Action Laboratory at NYU, one novice walker racked up an astonishing 69 falls per hour while learning to take those first formative steps (Adolph et al., 2012). While it is impressive enough that each child ultimately learned how to walk, it may be more impressive that these infants did not give up. What drives the smallest of our species to persist at a task against such brutal feedback? Likely there's someplace exciting to be, something new to explore, or in our home, delicious dog toys my boys eagerly sought out to chomp down upon.

As humans, we're born curious. Like very short scientists, we experiment on the world around us first by sticking things in our mouths and later by boldly barging forward upright towards ever more exciting adventures. This innate curiosity is what drives us to explore, engage, and learn about the world around us. Curiosity is the impetus for discovering what is safe and what is not and provides practice taking on roles that all young animals will inhabit as they grow.

When curiosity takes flight, we often call it *play*. In humans, play is critical in establishing foundational social, physical, and cognitive skills from literacy to cultural norms (Brooker, 2017). And that play is how we learn to navigate the complex social rules for engaging with others, how to be flexible in different situations, and even how to solve problems, no flash-cards necessary (Hirsh-Pasek, Golinkoff, & Eyer, 2004)! What's more, as we act on our environment through play we are learning about the boundaries of our world, the opportunities to innovate, and we find the ways where we fit in as well as where we can stand out.

The paradox of our current education system, then, is finding children sitting in rows to learn the same facts and figures at the very same time. They might achieve a score on a test, despite the best science supporting the critical role of explo-ration and play in learning. As a child I was afraid to chal-lenge the status quo; perhaps I learned through play that a good student sits still, receives knowledge, and moves along.

Compliance was my companion for many years until I finally wondered: why? The learning that transpired once I took hold of my own learning journey was inexplicably liberating. Learning for the joy of learning, trying on new words and theories and applying them in my classroom the next day was exhilarating. From business to education to research to inno-vation, I learned that I was starved for the freedom that play afforded. Unleashing my own curiosity has led down the windy path of realization that compliance is a boring fellow; I much prefer curiosity.

Adolph, K. E., Cole, W. G., Komati, M., Garciaguirre, J. S., Badaly, D., Lingeman, J. M., ... & Sotsky, R. B. (2012). How do you learn to walk? Thousands of steps and dozens of falls per day. *Psychological Science, 23*(11), 1387-1394.

Brooker, L. (2017). Learning to play, or playing to learn? Children's participation in the cultures of homes and settings. In *Young Children's Play and Creativity* (pp. 14-25). Oxfordshire, UK: Routledge.

Hirsh-Pasek, K., Golinkoff, R. M., & Eyer, D. (2004). *Einstein never used flash cards: How our children really learn--and why they need to play more and memorize less.* Emmaus, PA: Rodale Books.

Twitter: @lportnoy
LinkedIn: https://www.linkedin.com/in/lportnoy/
Book: Portnoy, L. (2019) Designed to Learn. Alexandria, VA. ASCD.
Episode #83: Lindsay Portnoy on Demystifying Learning http://bit.ly/episode83-portnoy

* * *

Embrace Creativity and Flow

When learners have a voice and choice in what and how they are learning, especially if it is about something they are passionate about or interested in, they jump in and can get lost in the task or project. This is called "Flow." When learners are in the Flow, you can notice, see, and hear the engagement. Sometimes Flow is quiet.

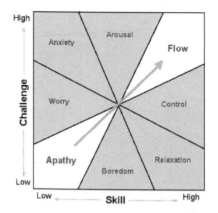

Fig. 8.2 Flow Chart - Csikszentmihalyi [Source: Adapted from Csikszentmihalyi, M. (1990). Flow: The Psychology of Optimal Experience. New York: Harper and Row.]

Mihaly Csikszentmihalyi is best known as the architect of the theory of Flow. Flow is when a person is fully immersed in what they are doing and there is a balance between the challenge of the task and the skill of the learner. Flow cannot occur if the task is too easy or too difficult.

Csíkszentmihályi published the graph above that depicts the relationship between the challenges of a task and skills. Flow only occurs when the activity is a higher-than-average challenge and requires above-average skills. Both skill level and challenge level must be matched and high; if skill and challenge are low and not matched, then apathy results (Csíkszentmihályi, 1996).

Activity about Flow

Reflect in your journal about different activities when you were in the "Flow."

- What were the activities? Was there one activity that stood out?

- How did you feel?
- What did you notice about time during those activities?
- When do you feel like that when you are learning something?

Engagement in Learning

Engagement is the affective side of learning and has been found to be a robust predictor of learner performance and behavior in the classroom (Martin-Kniep, 2012). Engagement refers to the degree of attention, curiosity, interest, optimism, and passion that learners show when they are learning. So this may mean "engagement" is about how much we learn in the classroom or anywhere we learn. I needed to explore this more, so I checked out the 2016 Gallup Student Poll that Dan Jackson mentioned in his story in Chapter 4. The poll helps educators gauge school success beyond test scores and grades. With nearly five million respondents since 2009, the 2016 survey helps educators provide a more positive school culture — one that builds engagement, creates hope for the future, fosters talent, and prepares students to meaningfully participate in the economy. Gallup Student Poll measures are linked to desirable learning outcomes, including self-reported grades, the perception of school success, and self-reported absenteeism.

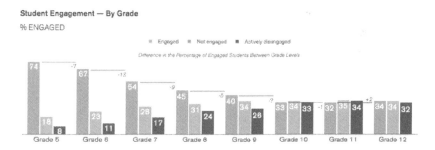

Fig. 8.3 Engagement by Grade

https://www.gallup.com/education/
227657/k12-education.aspx

Take a look at the 2016 snapshot report to learn more about how to empower hope and engagement in school. From the results, it is apparent in the Gallup Study that engagement decreased over the years in school. Yet, learning can happen anywhere and at any time, especially now with content available at our fingertips.

Pause/Think/Reflect

Some questions for you to consider when discussing engagement and to write what you find out in your journal:

- How much does the system have to do with encouraging or stopping curiosity, creativity, and engagement?
- What can we do to transform the system, so learners are more curious, creative, and engaged in learning?

Levels of Engagement

After learning about Flow and reviewing the Gallup report on engagement, I needed to see how it related to creativity based on Csíkszentmihályi's book and research. From what I learned about starting with the WHY, learners need to be motivated to want to learn first or they do what they are told to do and tend to be compliant. When we are in the "Flow," we are curious and want to be more creative and innovative. This doesn't always happen in "school," but it would be great if it did.

What I learned from the research and readings is that learners need to be intrinsically motivated to want to learn, to actually be engaged in the learning process. What they are learning and how they respond might be different in school than outside of school. Watch kids playing driven by wonder as Lindsay Portnoy wrote earlier in this chapter. Let's say they were curious about something they are passionate about or a game they were playing. They may be pushing and supporting each other to build a city in Minecraft. They may even forget to stop to eat. This is "Flow."

Refer to my post on Levels of Engagement for more information on learner engagement and how learners can be compliant in some situations and Flow in another situation.

| http://bit.ly/levels-of-engagement

Activity about Engagement

Refer to the questions below by reflecting in your journal about engagement:

- Do we only measure learning that happens in a school?
- Are teachers or a school responsible for engaging the learners?

- Can teachers empower learners to want to be more engaged in learning?
- Have you noticed some learners more engaged than others?
- Could it be who the learners are that impacts their level of engagement?
- How does the environment impact the learning?
- What might keep some learners from being engaged in the learning process?

Experiential Learning

I've known Dr. Jackie Gerstein for a very long time and always learn from her. I knew right away when I first met her that I wanted to build our friendship. I had a wonderful conversation with Jackie on one of my earliest podcasts, Episode #8. Jackie is a prolific writer and backs up everything she shares with research. She is also an amazing friend whom I value and asked her to share her WHY. I love how she shared it in such an innovative way.

* * *

Being an Experiential-based Educator
By Jackie Gerstein Ed.D.

Historically, teachers teach the way they were taught. I want to change this. I am on a mission to encourage and assist teachers in designing learning experiences they wished they had as students. Seriously, how many would create lecture-based learning settings? It is my belief that since that was the model used from early on, that most got used to it. Some tolerated it, some endured, and some dropped-out (dropping out does not necessarily mean physically, it can mean physically attending school but mentally dropping out). I was one of those who dropped out of school mentally and emotionally at a very young age.

At a workshop I attended, we were asked to write a letter to our younger selves. I wrote mine as if I was a teacher of a younger Jackie:

I will be an ethnographer in the study of you. I want to create learning experiences that invite you to disrupt, to innovate, to create, to imagine, to be you.
I will never make you listen to lectures of more than 15 minutes, memorize information, or take multiple-choice tests. You have told me that not only do you find these tasks boring, but you also find them painful. I will, instead, ask you to write, create, speak, make, and perform. I will ask you to experience your learning.

I know you find sitting in desks, sitting properly, sitting still to be confining, constricting, and contrived. Playing, moving, and tinkering are such integral parts of how you learn. Our learning environment will look more like a playroom or coffee shop than a classroom. Our playground will be an extension of our learning environment, not one separated by time and space.

Your need for wanting to know more about topics is inspiring. The Internet is such a gift for you. I will permit you to have your laptop open and search for information when the need arises. I will not ask you to unplug as you know when it is important to do. I will respect your ability to self-regulate. I will also ask you to share with others what you learn. I know you love to share what you find with others.

I know you "wonder" a lot out loud and ask a lot of questions including, "Why do I need to know this?" I will do my best to engage you in rich discourse or point you in directions where you can get answers to your questions. I promise not to "sssh" you as many teachers have. I know that it cuts through you like a knife and shuts down your passion and energy.

My "Why" for being an experiential-based educator early in my career which directly led to being a maker educator later in my career stems from not wanting learners to experience the pain I did as a K-12 student. Experiential and maker education helps learners tap into and amplify their passion for learning.

Episode #8 Podcast and Post: Framework for Maker Education with Dr. Jackie Gerstein
https://barbarabray.net/2017/08/24/framework-for-maker-education-with-dr-jackie-gerstein/
Jackie actively website/blog at https://usergeneratededucation.wordpress.com/
Jackie's New Book, Learning in the Making, can be accessed from her website (Gerstein, 2019)
Twitter handle: @jackiegerstein

* * *

Develop Your Passions to Discover What You Love and What You're Good At

We discussed your Passions in Chapter 6 on *ikigai*. You may not have fully realized what you love and what you are good at. Some of us know in our hearts what that is, but many of us think we know but question it. Yet, for many of us after pursuing that "passion," we find out later that it was the wrong direction. I thought dental hygiene was my passion. I mean, I devoted years of training, worked years with several dentists, and had over 300 clients who followed me from dentist to dentist. I must have been good at it. Right? Being good at dental hygiene didn't mean that I loved it. I stayed in the profession because I got accepted into the program. I was honored to be one out of 700 who got one of the 18 spots. How could I let them down and say I didn't want it? Like I said before, it was a great profession for me and paid me well, but something was missing. I found that out after I started teaching dental hygiene and working in my children's school that I loved to teach and learn more about computers. Actually, I was obsessed with computers. Now, I look back and realize that was my passion then. That's what "Flow" felt like. I know why I went into dental hygiene and don't regret a moment, but it wasn't my story. It was my guidance counselor's story for me. I guess I didn't know me well enough to say no. I rented her story to make it mine. Now I know better.

Watch/Pause/Reflect

| https://youtu.be/4_UlzOeF3Qg

Mentally Fragile to Mentally STRONG!
This motivational video with David Goggins shares that we tend to quit too quickly. Courage is like a muscle that gets stronger when we use it.

- Do you listen to others instead of listening to yourself?
- How can you choose response-ability for your life?

Adam's WHY

Adam Welcome, a principal in California, wrote *Kids Deserve It* with Todd Nesloney, a principal in Texas, about changing schools with their message. It was their manifesto to change the system NOW because kids deserve it. I've known Adam Welcome for years. We both live in the SF Bay area. In fact, I worked with his teachers to coach them as they created project-based learning activities using technology. When I first met Adam, I was impressed with his energy and dedication for teaching and learning. When I talked with Adam on my podcast for Episode #5, he had just written *Kids Deserve It* with Todd Nesloney. Now he's the author of three books and definitely an influencer. Adam is passionate about running and then decided to align his message with his message about schools. He did. He wrote *Run Like a Pirate*. Now his running has taken on a deeper meaning.

* * *

My WHY Has Changed
by Adam Welcome, author, speaker, principal

People that know me would call me a 'runner.'

I've run 30 marathons.

I've run a back and forth marathon where I ran the marathon course from the finish line to the starting line backwards during the middle of the night, and then turned around and ran the 'real' marathon with everyone else - 56.4 miles for the day.

I've run for 24 hours straight on New Year's Eve in 2017 and completed 103 miles in that time.

And then I ran a marathon with a little twist. I used to run for me, that was my **WHY**, but something changed last year.

Eight years ago I saw them for the first time, I was enamored and knew I wanted to be a part of what they were doing.

I applied, and I waited. I emailed about my application, and waited. I ran twenty marathons and still waited. And then the email came.

"Adam, we have a runner to match you up with for the upcoming marathon."

Up until that point, I was still running for me. My training was focused on a sub-3 hour marathon which is a really fast time and my runs hurt, but the training was going well.

When that email came, I scrapped everything, and my focus shifted.

How would I do this new race? What needed to happen for me to prepare? What would it be like for 26.2 miles? I couldn't believe it was actually happening after trying for many years. The time had finally come—I was going to guide a blind runner for an entire marathon.

I run. They run. They're blind. I guide them. It's as simple as that.

Of all the thirty marathons I've run, the one where I guided a blind runner for 26.2 miles was the most rewarding race of my life.

And it changed my life forever.

My **WHY** has changed. I no longer run for myself, I run for others.

To guide them.

To help change them.

To inspire and motivate them.

To show them that they can do anything, and even what they thought was impossible.

We need each other on this planet in which we all live. You and I both need a team. Some members of your team will cheer you on. And some members of your team will be the vision you need in order to navigate this life that we're all living.

It's important to have a 'why'—and it's even more important to analyze your why, to adjust your why and to make sure your why includes others, because whatever you're doing, it's fun to help someone else with **THEIR** why!

Twitter: @mradamwelcome
Website: https://mradamwelcome.com/
Book: Welcome, A. (2018) Run Like a Pirate. San Diego, CA. Dave Burgess Consulting.
Episode #5 Podcast & Post: Running Because Kids Deserve It https://barbarabray.net/2017/08/02/running-because-kids-deserve-it-with-adam-welcome/

* * *

Just like Adam wrote that kids deserve it, so do you. If you are not sure what your passion is or if you have a story to tell, take the time to explore what you love and are good at. You deserve it.

Activity: Brainstorm and Prioritize Your Passions

Consider these four key ground rules when brainstorming:

- There are no dumb ideas. Period. ...
- Don't criticize your ideas. ...
- Build on all the other ideas. ...
- Reverse the thought of "quality over quantity."

Take what you wrote in Chapter 6 on *ikigai* and in Chapter 7 on empathy about what you love and what you're good at and put those on post-it notes. Build on those ideas by writing as fast as you can more ideas or thoughts or questions on separate post-it notes placed on a board or flip chart. Then cluster similar notes together and add any other ideas that come to you.

Now stand back and review what you came up with. Ask yourself these questions:

- What makes you happy?
- What makes your heart sing?
- What excites you?
- What keeps you up at night?

Choose the top three to five ideas that could be the passion you want to develop. Then walk away and give yourself a day or so to think about them. When you come back, consider which one of these ideas you want to explore more.

 Happiness is not something ready-made. It comes from your actions."

— Dalai Lama

Questions to Ponder

- What does it mean for a child to be naturally curious? Why is play important for learning?

- What would you write in your letter to your younger self?
- What makes your heart sing? How can you do more of that?
- How do you express your gratitude? If you don't, when can you start sharing your gratitude?

Wonderings

I wonder if anyone knows what they really love when they are young. I've heard kids say they love a certain sport and take it up either during or after school. If they feel that they are not good enough or big enough or flexible enough, then they quit. I was a dancer and a gymnast. I loved it. I took modern dance, tap, jazz, ballet, and ballroom dance classes for twelve years. Since I'm short and used to be tiny, I just loved pushing myself. I thought dance would help me become a better gymnast and gymnastics would help me become a better dancer. I thought I was really good and that was what I loved. When I was in high school, I didn't make the gymnastics team. I tried out for a few dancing opportunities including auditioning as an extra in a movie. Didn't get picked. I thought I was a failure because I couldn't do what I loved. Instead of getting back up and trying again, I decided that I would look for something else to be me. Now, if you see me on the dance floor, you know I love dancing. That never stops. I always wondered if I had tried out for the gymnastics team another year, what would have happened? Now, at my age, please don't ask me to do a handstand or cartwheel.

 Did you know when you wonder you are learning?"

— MISTER ROGERS

* * *

If you are looking for additional resources and more about this chapter, go to:

- the book study questions, go to https://barbarabray.net
- digital resources, go to http://bit.ly/defineyourwhy-digital
- discussions on Twitter, use the hashtag #defineyourWHY

WHY ALIGN YOUR PASSION TO WHAT THE WORLD NEEDS?

> *There is no 'Plan B' because we do not have a 'Planet B.' We have to work and galvanize our action."*
>
> — UN SECRETARY-GENERAL BAN-KI MOON

Discovering Our Place in the World

When you work every day and have way too many commitments from your job, your family, and paying bills, there is little time left to focus on you. Times have changed. The world seems smaller. Just watching the news is overwhelming. Going online is like drinking from a firehose. We're in a different time when everything you may or may not want to hear is available on any device. I grew up with a black-and-white TV with four or five stations and only heard from a few perspectives about what was happening. Teachers were supposed to teach only from textbooks. Now we have multiple perspectives on different topics, it is easy to get confused about what to believe, teach, or learn. Are we being confused on purpose?

I needed to step back and really think about what we love and what the world needs. When I heard some people say that it is their time to take care of themselves and that they didn't have time to give back, I cringed. I do believe we have to take care of ourselves, but we don't have to put our heads in the sand. I was upset when I've heard people say that they didn't vote anymore because they said that their vote didn't make a difference. Oh my! What I mentioned as self-care in the previous chapter doesn't mean you have to forget that you are lucky to be alive. It is an honor to be a part of a community and a global citizen of the world.

Pause/Think/Reflect
There is a difference between self-care and isolating yourself.

You deserve to be happy and enjoy your life, but we are more than ourselves alone. I am in a different time in my life and have more time to enjoy my family and friends. I've been married a long time, and each year our love gets stronger. I'm trying to find time to be with my children and granddaughter more. I am grateful for my sisters because they share history with me and are very special to me. Any time I have with my mother-in-law who is 98 is such a gift. I make sure to reach out and spend time with my special friends. I have a large family that is growing and enjoy any time I have with them. I have unbelievable neighbors who watch out for each other. I have worked with amazing people who continue to support my dream and I support theirs. My circle has grown to include people from around the world. When I learned about the world with people from around the world, I realized how much these connections matter to me.

ME to WE

These circles in my life make me a stronger me. All of us have extended circles that move us from ME to WE.

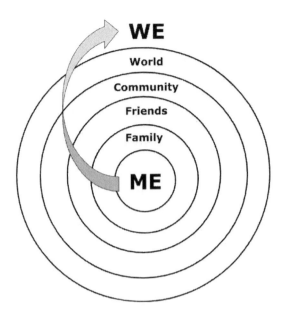

Fig. 9.1 Me to WE

> *We make a living by what we get. We make a life by what we give."*
>
> — Winston Churchill

This idea had me reflect on Maslow's hierarchy and self-actualization. With my work on personalized learning, I was focusing on the person and how they could become a self-directed, independent learner. Somehow community, culture, and ME to WE weren't discussed enough.

Maslow's Motivation Theory

I referred to Maslow's hierarchy of needs for as long as I can remember. I learned about it as a way of looking at the complete physical, emotional, social, and intellectual qualities of an individual, moving to self-actualization. I shared it during speeches, online, and in coaching. I never thought of where and how it came to be. I look back now and wish I had the curiosity and skepticism I have now and had done my research.

When I recently shared Maslow's hierarchy on Twitter, Ken Shelton sent me a direct message asking me if I had done research on Maslow's hierarchy. I asked him back "why?" He asked me to research the Maslow-Blackfoot connection. I did.

The article "Maslow's Hierarchy Connected to Blackfoot's Beliefs" by Karen Lincoln Michel in 2014 opened my eyes and reinforced some of my own thinking about what motivates people. Abraham Maslow as one of the founders of humanistic psychology "... generously borrowed from the Blackfoot people to refine his motivational theory on the hierarchy of needs."

Maslow's hierarchy of needs is a theory in psychology proposed by Abraham Maslow in his 1943 paper, "A Theory of Human Motivation" in *Psychological Review*. Maslow subsequently extended the idea to include his observations of humans' innate curiosity. Let me review with you what Maslow's theory suggests. He illustrates that people are motivated by fulfilling basic needs such as food, shelter, and clothing first, which is at the bottom of the triangle. As you move up the triangle, the next need is safety and security, then love and intimacy, then self-esteem, and then at the top: self-actualization. This highest level is where people are self-aware and achieve their fullest potential.

Fig. 9.2 Maslow's Hierarchy of Needs

 It is quite true that man lives by bread alone — when there is no bread. But what happens to man's desires when there is plenty of bread and when his belly is chronically filled? At once other (and "higher") needs emerge and these, rather than physiological hungers, dominate the organism. And when these in turn are satisfied, again new (and still "higher") needs emerge and so on. This is what we mean by saying that the basic human needs are organized into a hierarchy of relative prepotency."

— (MASLOW, 1943, P. 375)

In reading several reviews of the theory, I found several critical evaluations of the findings. Maslow used limited samplings of self-actualized people including biographies and writings of 18 people he identified as being self-actualized. He used personal opinion, which is prone to bias and reduces the validity of the data obtained. But that didn't seem to matter to educators. If you do a search on Maslow's hierarchy of needs, you will see this five-level version. There is a seven-stage and then an eight-stage model later developed during the 1960s and 1970s (McLeod, 2018).

Blackfoot Nation's tipi

Abraham Maslow visited the Blackfoot nation in Alberta, Canada in 1938. There is evidence of his work there with a link to an archival photo (http://www.albertaonrecord.ca/is-glen-3802) that places Maslow on the Blackfoot reserve at that time, and on the Blackfoot people's influence on him. Karen Michel (Michel, 2014) interviewed Dr. Cindy Blackstock who is the Executive Director of the First Nations Child and Family Caring Society of Canada about Maslow's connection to the Blackfoot Nation.

The Blackfoot belief is not a triangle. It is a tipi that reaches to the sky.

Self-actualization is at the base of the tipi, not at the top, and is the foundation on which community actualization is built. The highest form that a Blackfoot can attain is called "cultural perpetuity."

Blackstock (2011) shared in her research, the breath of life theory that was interpreted by Native American child welfare expert Terry Cross in the relational worldview model. The principles are categorized into four domains (cognitive, physical, spiritual, and emotional) of personal and collective well-being:

Cognitive: Self and community actualization, role, identity, service, esteem	**Physical**: Food, water, housing, safety, and security
Spiritual: Spirituality and life purpose	**Emotional**: Belonging and relationship

Table 9.1 Four Domains

Blackstock explained cultural perpetuity as something her Gitksan people call "the breath of life." It's an understanding that you will be forgotten, but you have a part in ensuring that your people's important teachings live on.

Blackstock referred to research by Ryan Heavy Head and Red Crow Community College on the Blackfoot approach to science funded through a SSHRC Aboriginal Research Grant shared in a post in 2007, "How First Nations Helped Develop a Keystone of Modern Psychology."

 Blackfoot people have their own systems for developing new knowledge in traditional ways. It's less focused on categories and more interested in how things come together."

— Ryan Heavy Head, researcher, Red Crow

As illustrated in Blackstock's diagram below, self-actualization was on the bottom, as the starting point. The self was only the beginning for the Blackfoot, who placed community actualization and cultural continuity above the individual. Maslow's western lens flipped it around to prioritize the individual (Johnson, 2018).

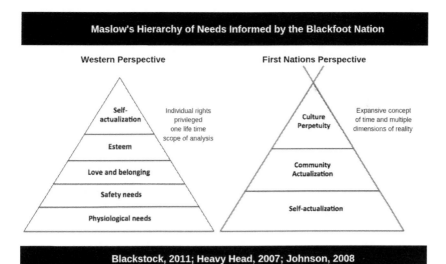

Fig. 9.3 Maslow's Hierarchy Informed by the Blackfoot Nation

The graphic above of the basic differences between Western and First Nations perspectives is a recreation of the graphic presented by University of Alberta professor Dr. Cindy Blackstock at the 2014 conference of the National Indian Child Welfare Association.

Community and Connections Matter

After realizing how Maslow's Hierarchy was informed by the Blackfoot Nation, I could see how self matters, but community and culture make us whole and make us who we are. We cannot live alone. ME to WE. Culture and community matter. The connections I made through my work with my podcast, my writing, and this book brought me to this time. I realized I could not do what I do alone. I go to social media to keep up with the latest technology and research. I wanted to create a podcast that focused on the person I was having the conversation with, their journey, and their passions. I found out some things they never told anyone else. I found out how resilient people are and how their community and connections have helped them become who they are.

The Power of Connections

I have been fortunate to make awesome global connections through social media and conferences like ISTE (International Society for Technology in Education). I wrote the Professional Development (PD) column for 17 years for CUE (past known as Computer Using Educators) and, in 2000, I was on assignment to find unique stories about teacher PD around the world. I took on the challenge and decided to walk up to people I didn't know. I met twelve new educators and wrote the feature article. I still have the 2000 newsletter with that article and keep the connections going I made that year. In fact, I connected with Dr. Jay Cohen from WHYY Radio just last year in Philadelphia, who was my lead story—only 18 years later.

At the 2017 ISTE conference in San Antonio, Texas, I sat down at a table with a woman who was sitting by herself. I didn't know that initial connection would be powerful for both of us. When Ilene Winokur-Alzaid and I started talking, we didn't stop. We were both interested in each other's lives because we saw similarities and were learning about interesting stories that kept going deeper. We ended up connecting at the next two ISTEs, rooming together. I learned even more when Ilene was on Episode #41 on my podcast. We are taking a TED Masterclass as partners and hoping both of us can do a TED Talk. We found that our stories support each other as we discover our WHY.

* * *

The Power of Global Connections
By Dr. Ilene Winokur-Alzaid

I am not sure how my initial interest in connecting through social media started, but I remember I felt the need to know more about what educators in other countries were doing in their classrooms and schools. I have lived in Kuwait for the past 35 years and felt out of touch with "best practices" that could be applied to support my ELL students and make their learning more meaningful. My initial attempt at connecting was on Twitter. I lurked for a while until I felt more comfortable and knowledgeable about how to establish my online presence and make my time spent on it worthwhile.

I learned early on that educators love to share what they know and the resources they use in their own classrooms. I began to read posts about using the Sustainable Development Goals (SDGs) to teach a variety of concepts and content while showing students there is a whole world out there to connect with and learn from while helping to achieve goals that will help us all. At about the same time, I found out about the annual ISTE conference and began following some of the sessions that were either streamed live by #PasstheScopeEDU or tweeted out by my PLN. I was hooked!

I promised myself that I would attend ISTE the following year and became a member. Once I did, I found out about the ISTE Global Collaboration Network and volunteered as an "at large" member of the leadership team. During the first meeting I attended (virtually on Google Hangouts), the team was discussing how to encourage global collaboration rather than global connections. I suggested that it seemed logical to incorporate the SDGs in our planning, and the rest of the team agreed. Since then, many of the GCN's monthly webinars have focused on global collaboration and the SDGs.

My WHY has always been about helping others. It makes me feel good to know that I have made someone else's day or helped them solve a problem they were facing. Connecting online and finding ways to extend my empathic reach has supported my personal transitions from full-time mother and educator, to full-time educator with empty nest, to retired educator. My connections on Twitter have opened up a whole new world for me. My future plans are: training refugee teachers, using my expertise in teaching English to second language learners, and spreading understanding about the Kuwaiti and Arab cultures.

I am a lifelong learner. I continue to learn from everyone I connect with online, and I know the feeling is mutual; another part of my WHY. Connecting and finding my PLN has been life-changing. I continue to marvel at the power of our connections to support each other and establish friendships across the miles.

Twitter: @IleneWinokur
Website/Blog: http://eddilene.edublogs.org/

Episode #41 Podcast and Post: Supporting and Mentoring Teachers
http://bit.ly/episode41-winokur

* * *

The UN Sustainable Development Goals (SDGs)

The United Nations Foundation wrote about WHY they do what they do.

The UN is indispensable to tackling humanity's greatest challenges and driving global progress. Created out of the ashes of World War II, the UN works to unite countries against their greatest threats and in service of their highest aspirations. In its over 70 years, the UN has helped reduce conflict and maintain peace around the world, alleviate poverty, advance human rights, and deepen cooperation around shared purpose. As our world grows more connected and threats more complex, the UN remains essential to driving global progress. Because of the UN, all 193 Member States came together to agree on 17 Sustainable Development Goals – humanity's blueprint for a better world by 2030. (Source: Why the UN https://unfoundation. org/why-the-un/)

The 2030 Agenda for Sustainable Development (https:// sustainabledevelopment.un.org/), adopted by all United Nations Member States in 2015, provides a shared blueprint for peace and prosperity for people and the planet, now and into the future. At its heart are the 17 Sustainable Development Goals (SDGs), which are an urgent call for action by all countries—developed and developing— in a global partnership. They recognize that ending poverty and other deprivations must go hand-in-hand with strategies that improve health and education, reduce inequality, and spur economic growth—all while tackling climate change and working to preserve our oceans and forests.

| Fig. 9.4 Sustainable Development Goals

<u>All the resources from a variety of sites are free for you</u>. You do not have to be a teacher to use any of the resources or take any of the free courses they offer. If you share these resources with children, it helps them become aware of what others around the world are doing to make change about real-world issues. You can refer to it in whole or use it in parts depending on what you want to learn or teach. There are children around the world who are taking action on multiple issues especially the urgency to meet SDG 13: Climate Action.

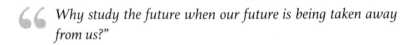 *Why study the future when our future is being taken away from us?"*

— GRETA THUNBERG, STUDENT ACTIVIST

The World's Largest Lesson

You can then review the introductory World's Largest Lesson that introduces the SDGs to children and young people everywhere and unites them in action. There are free resources, projects, and activities available that anyone can use. The first lesson is for anyone to introduce the global goals. You can put yourself on the map to become part of the story uniting a generation to change the world by 2030. First, explore the map and then click Become Part of the Story. (http://worldslargestlesson.globalgoals.org)

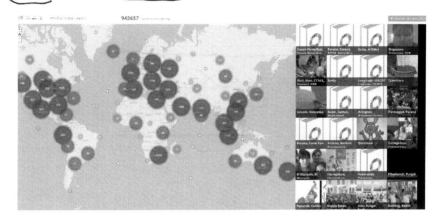

| Fig. 9.5 World's Largest Lesson Map

Not only are there these lessons, projects, and resources; there are facts and figures, comics, videos, stories, and ways to connect to others around the world.

Check out and join in another resource that curates projects and lesson: The Goals Project at https://www.goalsproject.org/2019-goals-projects.html. In 2019, I became a #TeachSDGs Ambassador Cohort 3 because I wanted to learn and share more resources with educators around the world. You can become an ambassador at https://teachsdgs.org.

Going Deeper with the SDGs Targets and Indicators

With the 17 goals, there are 169 targets and additional indicators for each goal. When I work with teachers, I realize the goals are just a starting point. I take them deeper by choosing a target and identifying an indicator that they can work on and try to meet by a specific time.

The Human Rights Guide to the Sustainable Development Goals (http://sdg.humanrights.dk/) designed by the Danish Institute for Human Rights illustrates the human rights anchorage of the 17 Sustainable Development Goals (SDGs) by making concrete links between the 169 targets and the relevant range of:

- International and regional human rights instruments
- International labour standards
- Key environmental instruments - some of which have human rights dimensions

The Guide provides a list of instruments to support the work people can do around the goals and support them in meeting the targets.

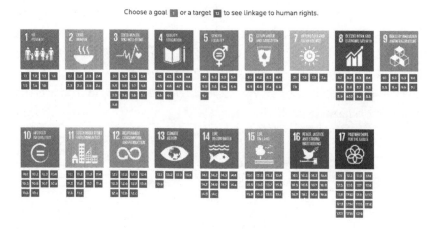

| Fig. 9.6 Human Rights Guide to SDGs and Targets

This resource has helped me do my research and share ideas with teachers and others who are interested in meeting the SDGs by 2030. Below is an example of one goal with one target and the indicator to use to measure progress.

Goal 4: Quality Education. Ensure inclusive and equitable quality education and promote lifelong learning opportunities for all.

Target 4.4. By 2030, substantially increase the number of youth and adults who have relevant skills, including technical and vocational skills, for employment, decent jobs and entrepreneurship.

Indicator 4.4.1. Proportion of youth and adults with information and communications technology (ICT) skills, by type of skill

Empathy to Impact

I met Steve Sostak on Twitter after he and his co-director, Aaron Moniz started Inspire Citizens. I was following his journey and what he was doing in China and wanted to learn more. We decided we needed to talk, and I was fortunate to have a wonderful conversation with both of them. What they are doing around *Empathy to Impact* is now going global. I invited Steve to guest host the #rethink_learning Twitter chat around the global competency theme. Now Steve and Aaron are taking their message globally. They are making a difference by doing a hands-on student-centered approach with teachers around the SDGs and targets. I asked Steve if he would share his story. This is an excerpt from his amazing journey that I am honored to share with you.

* * *

Inspire Citizens' Empathy to Impact
By Steve Sostak

My journey started in 2005 when my wife, Angie, and I decided to leave Chicago for Lima, Peru. We wanted to trade challenges of inner-city schools for new challenges in international teaching. In 2007, I taught grade four in Lima when Angie was four-months pregnant and when we adopted our two Peruvian daughters, Jessica (15) and Maria (5).

This was clearly a major event for us. Then we moved to Malaysia and then China. This incredible journey led me to become more globally competent, transforming my life and work by opening a world of possibilities and learning from my students from different cultures and contexts.

There are many turning points in personal histories—causes, effects, changes, continuities, perspectives, successes, failures, elation, suffering. The time in Peru centered me; it was the birth of my vocation, a calling to link my personal strengths and talents to the needs of others outside of myself. I knew then, as a teacher, my students and I could positively and deeply impact communities beyond the walls of our classroom. Helping students to find their own vocations through projects and service amplified learning in powerful ways. Rooted in community engagement, deep thinking, relevant solutions, and impact on personal happiness and the well-being of others and the planet, *Empathy to Impact* became an idea that grew in my mind.

I quickly realized that this teaching style didn't have to fight against the expectations of existing academic standards. In fact, my students were more engaged, finding relevance in applying their skills to things they cared about and grew more than projected. I began utilizing the *Empathy to Impact* approach more. Parents and administrators saw kids that were dedicated to their greater community, were leaders and kinder to one another, and were thriving academically. But frustratingly, the teaching approach tended to stay pocketed in my classroom or in classrooms of a few other colleagues.

In 2018, I stepped away from day-to-day teaching to launch *Inspire Citizens* in China, traveling globally to share this educational mission along with an incredible friend, co-teacher, and co-director, Aaron Moniz.

Being in classrooms was always wonderful for Aaron and me, but we knew we could have a greater impact if we took the leap to create something with a wider reach, connecting with educators and students around the world with hopes of building diverse relationships necessary to transform education and make our collective future more sustainable.

At the core, *Inspire Citizens* supports schools to take the strengths of what is already happening and reframes community mindsets and student-centered learning experiences for greater empathy and impact, all linked to the application of existing standards. For partner schools, we apply best-practices in professional learning to contextualize and delve deep over time in attaining a Global Impact School status, supporting everything from pedagogical growth, to student leadership, to media for good programs, to unit planning, to training the trainers.

More schools are calling for deeper service learning and action opportunities. By using such tools as the United Nations Sustainable Development Goals (SDGs), all teachers can help kids link what they love and are good at with some of the world's greatest identified needs. For Inspire Citizens, we now call that framework *Talent + Target = Vocation.*

Teachers and students are coached to work in a service-learning, PBL, or inquiry cycle that is enhanced by a dedication to deeper thinking and action. And student outcomes center on global competencies rooted in civics, citizenship, service, and good, but also in the context of each community. Our *Student Impact Profile* is being adapted by numerous schools internationally as a graduate profile, highlighting pathways for students to make a greater impact for collective wellbeing and sustainable development while applying skills and learning more about the potential of humanity.

In the end, as educators, we have to ask ourselves, what is the purpose of school? What's our vocation? My goal and my WHY has always been to help my students find learning relevant, be well, positively impact the world, and experience life through their own journey, transforming futures in a way that I did beginning in 2005.

Co-Director, Inspire Citizens https://inspirecitizens.org/
Twitter: @inspirecitizen1 #EmpathytoImpact
Email: steve@inspirecitizens.org

* * *

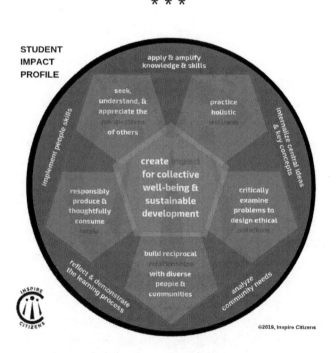

| Fig. 9.7 Inspire Citizens's Student Impact Profile

Kids with the SDGs

I learned about Darren Ellwein @dellwein on Twitter years ago, and I knew I needed to learn more about this principal from South Dakota.

When Darren was attending a Google Summit in California, he was close enough for us to connect and realized we had similar goals for kids and teachers. Then we set up times to talk about personalized learning via appear.in, a cool video conferencing program. After he was on my podcast, I couldn't believe all his school was doing to personalize learning and the connections Darren had made. I'll let Darren tell his story about the SDGs.

* * *

Empower Kids with the SDGs
By Darren Ellwein

At South Middle School in Harrisburg, South Dakota, we always work to bring authentic, real experiences to our learners. Our personalized learning program allows kids to create their schedules daily based on differentiated offerings from facilitators. Adding more juice to personalized learning in our school, I added Stanford's design thinking model to an experience that focuses on the UN Sustainable Development Goals (SDGs).

The class is called Impact because we believe that 11-14 year-olds can impact our world to bring or create change for the better. How do you create such a class? You provide a flexible framework for learners to follow and get out of the way. Kids need to feel empowered to create their direction. They need adults who can facilitate, but who understand the boundaries of ownership. They need adults who let them struggle with their ideas, provide insight and direction at key moments in the process, and teach kids how to communicate their ideas clearly.

SDGs fit perfectly with a personalized learning framework because the goals are diverse enough to ignite a passion in every learner. Steve Sostak is the igniter in the early stages of their learning. He visits each class, explaining the purpose of the goals and his work around the world. He brings the world to our classroom in South Dakota. Once the learners have researched the tiles or SDGs, they select a tile, drill down to a specific target in the goal, and use the design thinking process to bring their learning to life. Relationship is the purpose of our school and a primary component in Impact. As they work on their goal and target, the kids have to find an expert on that goal. Our kids have had experts from Morocco, Nigeria, China, Thailand, the United States, and many more places. One project included a learner working with Soi Dog in Thailand to stop the dog and cat meat trade in parts of the world. Another project brought gender equity to light by our girls connecting with girls from a village in Nigeria.

The next step for our learners is a class that will allow them to create their own business or nonprofit that will bring their SDG work to the world. These types of classes are my WHY - empower kids to drive their learning with creativity and authentic experiences.

Episode #23 Podcast & Post: Inspiring Kids to Greatness with Darren Ellwein https://goo.gl//KuDCyB
Twitter: @dellwein
Website: Under the Influence: https://edtransformed.wordpress.com/
Book: Ellwein, D. & McCoy, D. The Revolution (2019) San Diego, CA: Dave Burgess Consulting.

* * *

 However, I continue to try, and I continue, indefatigably, to reach out. There's no way I can single-handedly save the world or, perhaps, even make a perceptible difference—

but how ashamed I would be to let a day pass without making one more effort."

— Isaac Asimov

Teach SDGs Ambassador

When I learned about the UN Global Goals that are the Sustainable Development Goals (SDGs), I had to be involved and became a TeachSDGs Ambassador in Cohort 3. I remember asking audiences in the U.S. in 2016 and 2017 who knew about the UN Goals, and no one raised their hands. I realized then that my job was to bring awareness of the SDGs to teachers so they could empower learners to collaborate globally and act locally. I am fortunate to be a Teach-SDGs Ambassador (teachsdgs.org) along with many inspirational educators from around the world, including JoAnn Jacobs, who is an eighth-grade teacher at Mid-Pacific Institute in Honolulu, Hawaii. I have known JoAnn since 2009, when I worked with her school on Project-Based Learning projects. I visited her class and knew right away that JoAnn is an amazing teacher. We have been friends ever since. JoAnn has written guest posts for my website about the global collaboration projects and been on my podcast. I asked JoAnn if she would share her WHY about the SDGs.

* * *

The UN Global Goals
By JoAnn Jacobs

For the past four years, the United Nations Sustainable Development Goals or Global Goals have been a part of my curriculum. This is solely by choice and not by mandate. The question then becomes, why the goals and not something else? The reason, or my WHY, is why not?

When I first became involved with this topic, the changes taking place on Earth were called Global Warming, which many felt only involved temperature change. Now, with greater information, the name of the topic is currently Climate Change, which encompasses more than just temperature change. It involves the world's population and what is necessary for them to have a life worth living not only for themselves but for their families.

I ask my students to look at the world globally as opposed to only looking at their own backyard because it's more than a subject or a grade—it's their future.

Truthfully, I feel if I did not incorporate the goals into my curriculum, I would be doing my students a great disservice. The goals not only open their eyes as far as the issues but also to humanity and impresses upon them the knowledge that many in the world are not as fortunate as they are. I do not preach but open the door, knowing not everyone will walk through. It is a choice given to each one of my students. The seed is planted; it might grow today, it might grow years later, or not at all, and that's okay.

My WHY also stems from being a child of the 60s. I saw and experienced growing up and continually wondered, "why is this happening?" I have always been involved in my community even during the twenty years my husband was in the Navy. It is a part of my DNA. I would not be whole if I could not help those around me. This is My WHY, this is me, and I wouldn't want it to be any other way.

Twitter handle: @JoAnnJacobs68
Episode #23 Podcast and Post: Global Collaboration Projects
https://barbarabray.net/2017/10/11/global-collaboration-projects-with-joann-jacobs/

* * *

Activity: Design Thinking with the SDGs

After learning about the SDGs, use the design thinking process to identify one Global Goal related to a problem or issue happening with an authentic audience and go deeper to address an existing lesson or project and align it with one of the targets. Your focus can be a local or global connection.

Empathize	Identify and write why you chose a specific audience and a problem around one of the Global Goals. Why is the problem, goal, or audience important to you?

Connect the problem the audience is having with one of the targets under the goal. Do deeper research about the problem.

Define	Discuss the target(s) for this goal. Define one target to research deeper. Explain why you chose that target and your plan to meet the target.

Review and brainstorm existing lessons or projects that align with the goal and target. If you don't have one that addresses the target, you may want to review and brainstorm lessons or projects at https://www.globaleducationconference.org/page/global-education-resources.

Ideate	Brainstorm with your partner existing lessons and projects or more ideas that are on the UN SDGs site that might address the target you chose.

After reviewing the target, choose one, and then select one lesson or project that aligns with that target. Consider what approach you want to include and invite student voice.

Prototype	Choose a lesson or project to start designing an approach that meets the target you chose and invites student voice and choice.

After you create your prototype, share it with others. You can also think about sharing after you implement the lesson or project.

Test	Share your prototype with other teachers. Reflect on the feedback you received and how you plan to implement the prototype.

Questions to Ponder

- Why is it important for all of us to be aware of the global goals?
- Why does culture matter? How does being part of community help meet the global goals?
- How can you align any of the UN SDGs and targets with what you teach or are doing now?
- How are you connecting with others beyond your own community?

Wonderings

 Be a global citizen. Act with passion and compassion. Help us make this world safer and more sustainable today and for the generations that will follow us. That is our moral responsibility."

— UN Secretary-General, Ban Ki-moon (Korea)
who served from January 2007 to December 2016

All of us are citizens of the world. Kids of all ages may not know they can make a difference. The UN SDGs make us aware of issues that are happening globally and impact us locally. Yet, when I asked my audiences how many know about the SDGs, very few raised their hands. I have found out as a TeachSDGs Ambassador that more educators are getting involved and connecting with other classrooms around the world. I hope you join the movement and bring your students along.

> " *I alone cannot change the world, but I can cast a stone across the waters to create many ripples.*"
>
> — MOTHER TERESA

* * *

If you are looking for additional resources and more about this chapter, go to:

- the book study questions, go to https://barbarabray.net
- digital resources, go to http://bit.ly/defineyourwhy-digital
- discussions on Twitter, use the hashtag #defineyourWHY

WHY YOUR PASSION CAN BE YOUR MESSAGE AND YOUR WHY?

Be genuine. Be remarkable. Be worth connecting with."

— SETH GODIN

Hopes and Dreams

ope is about being optimistic with expectations of positive outcomes about specific events and circumstances in your life. Parents have hope for their children. Teachers have hope for the kids in their classrooms. Administrators have hope for everyone in the school community. We need to be optimistic because every child deserves whatever it takes for every child.

Hope video:
https://youtu.be/dlcU5uHMdTM

Watch/Reflect/Journal

This video from Parkway Schools when they asked students and teachers one question:
What is Your Hope?

Dreams are different from hopes. Dreams are fantasies created with a mixture of imagination and play. Most of us define our dreams as practically unachievable, and consequently, we aren't attached to their fruition.

 Hope is the dream of a waking man.

— ARISTOTLE

My One Word

All of us have hopes and dreams. My friends on Twitter asked us to come up with our One Word for 2019. When I wrote this post "My One Word for 2019" about what 2019 would hold for all of us, I thought about how each new year holds endless possibilities. Instead of "Impossible," I saw, "I'm possible." I didn't see it until now. I love this word: "Possibilities." I see us considering "Possibilities" to achieve our hopes and dreams. http://bit.ly/oneword-possibilities

 Nothing is impossible. The word itself says I'm possible!"

— AUDREY HEPBURN

Choosing My One Word for 2020 was an interesting exercise for me since I've been writing this book. I brainstormed ideas for one possible word for the year: stories, hope, purpose, why, believe, be, responsibility, gratitude, and more. This year is exciting for me with the focus on WHY and stories. I couldn't write this book without the support of my family, friends, and colleagues. I am so grateful. That's it! My #OneWord for 2020 is GRATITUDE. 2020 will be the year I have an Attitude for Gratitude. http://bit.ly/oneword-gratitude

Fig. 10.1 My One Word 2020

Activity: Your One Word

Create your One Word for 2020 and include the hashtag #One-Word2020. You can share it on Twitter and tag me using my handle @bbray27. I'll have a place on my companion website http://bit.ly/

defineyourwhy-digital for you to share your one word and a post on my website, https://barbarabray.net to share mine.

- Think about your hopes, dreams, and what you came up as your *ikigai*.
- Come up with One Word for the new year and add the hashtag #OneWord2020.
- Create a graphic that depicts your One Word.
- Share your One Word on Twitter and Instagram or whatever way feels good for you

I hope for peace, love, and compassion I hope we see more random acts of kindness. I hope to share all the kind actions taken by people in my #PLN (Personal Learning Network). Thank you, Tamara Letter, @tamaraletter, Hans Appel @HansNAppel, and many more who spread kindness and shared stories. I see possibilities for kindness around the world. I asked people on Twitter what was their WHY and Barbara Gruener, who was on my Rethinking Learning podcast, shared it beautifully.

* * *

My WHY
by Barbara Gruener

My WHY? People. Plain and simple. Connecting with them, uplifting them, listening to them, feeling empathy, showing compassion, sharing kindness, being in the moment with them, delighting in their presence, building hope, loving them unconditionally, making them ALL my favorite.

Excerpt from conversation on podcast:
To me, SEL (social-emotional learning) and Character Development are all about how we establish and maintain healthy relationships, about communicating, self-regulating, making

responsible decisions, connecting relationally. It's HEART work, it's holy work, and it's important work. It's also about serving, about being the KIND of leader that we would follow. It's about head, heart, and hands; it starts with empathy, becomes compassion, then moves to kindness. And kindness, my friends, is the real global warming!

Twitter: @BarbaraGruener
Barbara's website/blog: https://:corneroncharacter.com
Book: Gruener, B. (2014) What's Under Your Cape. Northville, MI.
Ferne Press
Episode #82: Connecting by Heart with Barbara Gruener
http://bit.ly/episode82-gruener

* * *

I dream about a world that uses empathy and finds ways to help people who are struggling. I plan to find more stories or seek them out on social media, through projects, and from EDUheroes, students, and thought leaders who take risks to help others. We are on this planet together. We need to be there for each other. We can dream big, look at real-world problems, and design activities that make a difference. Dream with me. You can believe in all the possibilities. Just look at the kids who started #MarchforourLives and are protesting for #ClimateAction. Both are now international movements. Nothing can stop them now.

 Go confidently in the direction of your dreams. Live the life you have imagined."

— Henry David Thoreau

Becoming the Best YOU

When I first moved to California, my dad found a job for me at the Parks Job Corps Center in Pleasanton, California, where he was comptroller. That first summer in California right after I graduated from high school was so lonely for me that having a job there helped me see how lucky I really was. I had no idea of my future or what I wanted to do with my life. Being a receptionist in the medical center there introduced me to young men who were struggling, and the Job Corps was possibly their last chance. I took my life for granted and met some amazing people who opened my eyes to what struggle really was. That's when I met George Foreman.

I was almost 19 when George became a close friend of our family. He was at the Job Corps in northern California, where my dad worked. I knew him then as someone who was very humble and still is. He has continued to be a big part of our family. I asked George if he would write a short vignette about his WHY and what that meant for his journey.

* * *

Becoming the Best ME
By George Foreman

My life growing up had been defined by the names I'd been called, even in my home. It continued all the way through school and the playground. Then one day, the first time I was far away from home at the Job Corps in Grants Pass, Oregon, I heard this speech: "*Some of you are angry and getting into fights. It's probably because of the names you are called. Just know that you are an American. That's who you are. An American! No one can ever take that away from you.*"

When I heard that, it changed me. My anger disappeared. I

learned that being patriotic and being called an American meant that I could become the best ME I could be. I'm proud that I've had the opportunities and successes I've had. Being an American. That's my WHY!

George Foreman
Olympic Gold Medalist, Two-Time Heavyweight Champion of the World and King of the Grill

* * *

My dad was not only the comptroller; he was a coach for the wrestling and boxing teams at Parks Job Corps Center. Dad said to us that one of the young men on the boxing team there was going to be the Heavyweight Champion someday. That big sweet boxer who he brought home to meet the family was George. We followed his journey as he proudly waved the American flag when he became the U.S. Olympic Champion in 1968, Heavyweight Champion twice, successful salesman and entrepreneur, philanthropist, and an ordained minister of his own church in Houston, Texas. He continued his friendship with my parents through my sister, Sandy, and me. George shares my belief in the value of education, and over the years, he has encouraged me in my efforts to support educators.

In 2008, when both my parents were seriously ill, my family life in turmoil, and I almost lost my house and my business, George reached out to me, listened, and coached me to get back up and keep punching. He has always inspired me to never give up, told me to "Feel the POWER," and to fight for what I believe. Thank you, George!

Personal Bill of Rights

I thought about what George told me about feeling the power when I took on any challenge. Barbara Gruener shared her personal rights on Twitter and posted them on her website (https://

corneroncharacter.blogspot.com/2018/07/my-personal-bill-of-rights.html).

She challenged her friends, including me, on Twitter, to come up with a list of our own personal bill of rights, and I did. http://bit.ly/personal-rights-bray

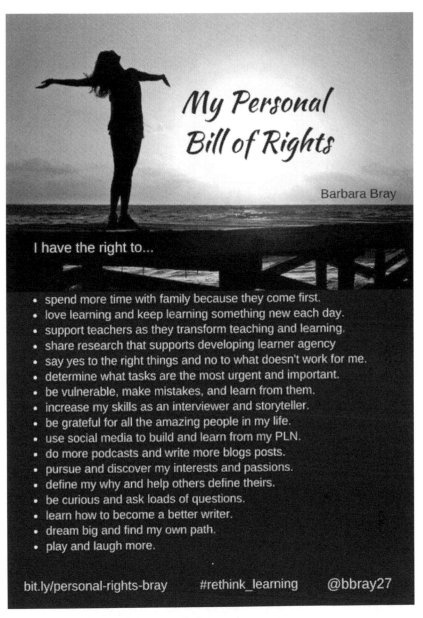

My Personal Bill of Rights

Barbara Bray

I have the right to...

- spend more time with family because they come first.
- love learning and keep learning something new each day.
- support teachers as they transform teaching and learning.
- share research that supports developing learner agency
- say yes to the right things and no to what doesn't work for me.
- determine what tasks are the most urgent and important.
- be vulnerable, make mistakes, and learn from them.
- increase my skills as an interviewer and storyteller.
- be grateful for all the amazing people in my life.
- use social media to build and learn from my PLN.
- do more podcasts and write more blogs posts.
- pursue and discover my interests and passions.
- define my why and help others define theirs.
- be curious and ask loads of questions.
- learn how to become a better writer.
- dream big and find my own path.
- play and laugh more.

bit.ly/personal-rights-bray   #rethink_learning   @bbray27

| Fig. 10.2 My Personal Bill of Rights

I started with 24 rights and then whittled it down to 17. I definitely know that these will change as I learn more about myself. I found this image on Pixabay.com that goes with my feelings about these rights. I will be adding "jumping for joy" in the future because I see more joy in my future. I also will be adding "balance" because I need to work less and play more. Life is just too short to not take the time to enjoy it.

Activity: Create your Personal Bill of Rights

Look for an image that represents you on Pixabay, Pexels, or other free picture collections. Use a program like Canva, Buncee, or Google Drawing to create your Personal Bill of Rights.

- Pixabay https://pixabay.com/
- Pexels https://www.pexels.com/discover/
- Canva https://www.canva.com/
- Buncee https://app.edu.buncee.com/

Reflect in your journal by responding to the following questions to take the challenge to write your own personal Bill of Rights.

- What would yours say if you took the time to write one?
- What do you have the right to . . . and to be free from?
- Start with 20-25 rights and then whittle it down to 15-ish.

Share your personal Bill of Rights, on your blog, on Twitter, or on my companion website: http://bit.do/defineyourwhy-digital. Make sure you tag your Bill of Rights with your handle and the hashtag #defineyourWHY.

Align Beliefs with Your Passion

I didn't know what sketchnoting was until Sylvia Duckworth created a graphic for George Couros for his book, *The Innovator's Mindset* (Couros, 2015). I reached out to George and asked him how he created that graphic. He introduced me to Sylvia. It wasn't long before my friendship with Sylvia grew, and she created graphics for Personalize

Learning, LLC. Sylvia was very generous with her time and worked with me late into many nights, helping me revise my ideas and drawings I did in Google Drawings and then edited with Kathleen. Now just for your information, I live in California, and Sylvia lives in Toronto, Canada, three time zones apart. At one point, I saw it was 11 pm my time, and we were still working. I saw how passionate she was about sketchnoting and teaching others how to sketchnote. In fact, she has two wonderful books on sketchnoting. I learned more about her and her journey in our Episode #32 podcast. I treasure our friendship and enjoy following her journey as a sketchnoter, author, speaker, and friend.

* * *

Sketchnoting
By Sylvia Duckworth

I first learned about sketchnoting around 2012, when I started to notice some beautiful drawings on social media related to education. I found out they were called sketchnotes, and since I was intrigued, I decided to give it a try on my iPad.

When I first started sketchnoting, I had zero confidence in my drawing abilities. I devoured any information I could find on the internet about how to sketchnote, and I worked really hard on building my visual vocabulary. I learned about different elements of sketchnoting, such as how to draw containers, frames, connectors, dividers, different fonts, and how to draw simple people and animals and lots of different icons. I practiced daily to improve my skills using online resources and various books (see resource list here - http://bit.ly/sketchnoting4teachers-duckworth.

Eventually, I became brave enough to post some of my drawings on social media in 2013. I was astonished to realize that people were admiring my work and sharing amongst themselves. This was positive reinforcement for me, and I continued to work on my developing my sketchnoting skills and to create more sketchnotes related to education. Sketchnoting most definitely did become a passion of mine. I loved the challenge of turning a concept into a drawing that people could easily understand and relate to.

Today, I have retired after 32 years of teaching, and I travel around the world to teach people about the joys and benefits of sketchnoting. This has definitely become my "WHY" in the past couple of years. I'm thrilled that sketchnoting has caught the attention of educators around the world and that they are sharing their enthusiasm for it with their students.

I wrote my first book, *Sketchnotes for Educators,* because I wanted to create a collection of my most popular sketchnotes to share with other educators. My second book, called *How to Sketchnote: A Step-By-Step Manual for Teachers and Students*, was designed to help teachers introduce sketchnoting to their students in a very scaffolded manner.
(Duckworth, S. 2019)

I believe that sketchnoting is a great way to share any message because it allows anyone, even "non-artists," to creatively organize their thoughts and to present and capture their ideas in an original and meaningful way. I blog and share teaching resources at https://sylviaduckworth.com
Facebook: https://www.facebook.com/sylvia.duckworth.1/
Twitter: https://twitter.com/sylviaduckworth/
Instagram: https://www.instagram.com/sylviaduckworth/
Pinterest: https://www.pinterest.com/sylviaduckworth/

Sketchnoting Resources: http://bit.ly/sketchnoting4teachers and also
(Duckworth, 2019)

Episode #32 Podcast & Post: Connect, Collaborate, Create https://goo.gl/8raU1Z

* * *

Fig. 10.3 Creativity by Sylvia Duckworth

Create your Brand to Represent your Purpose

When you have a passion and purpose that you believe is driving you now, you need to let people know. In doing that, you will need to create and brand your message that represents your purpose. After having a conversation with Hans Appel on my podcast, I wanted to learn more about the Award Winning Culture he shared with me on the post that goes with Episode #54. Hans's story is about developing and fueling JOY to inspire kids. His story represents his passion and purpose.

* * *

Award-Winning Joy
By Hans Appel

Several years ago, I had the pleasure of meeting two game-changing educators that would go on to have a profound influence on me. John Norlin and Houston Kraft, co-founders of a whole child program called CharacterStrong, burst into my educational life with panache, positivity, and purpose. CharacterStrong is quite simply the best professional development training I've ever experienced because it helped me become reacquainted with my own WHY: Inspiring others to discover and develop their JOY. By combining Social-Emotional Learning with Character Ed, the creators have melded the best of both worlds into something absolutely revolutionary.

Creating a culture where students can find purpose and passion by bringing amazingness into the world through Character Strong helped me fuel my own joy.

Teaching our students, staff, and community the power of kindness, service, and empathy over time has helped us to intentionally transform Enterprise Middle School (Aka Wildcat Nation) into an award-winning culture. EMS was awarded the 2018 ASCD Whole Child Award for the state of Washington, 2018 Global Class Act Award for Kindness, and a 2019 PBIS Film Festival Finalist (including taking the top prize for the Community, Staff, and Parent category).

With an intentional focus on teaching students to find real meaning at school, we began to notice that there was a powerful band of highly driven student rockstars who desperately wanted to have a deeper impact on the world. Following an inspirationally-filled leadership conference (SERVUS Conference), my wife (Jennifer) and I decided to amplify student voice through a student-led leadership podcast. We believed that building a platform for these students to explore topics like Character, Excellence, and Community might allow them to further discover, reflect, and apply their passion for servant leadership. In truth, we had no idea how to podcast, if our students could do it, or if this giant risk-taking adventure would blow up in our face. But armed with a desire to create a more innovative approach to whole-child education, with an authentic audience, we spent the summer getting ready to cannonball into the deep end of personalized learning.

Our student-led leadership podcast, Award-Winning Culture (http://www.awardwinningculture.com/podcast), has been a SMASHING success of student agency. The Award-Winning Culture podcast has had the pleasure of interviewing athletes, authors, speakers, actors, educators, and celebrities. As their confidence has grown, our students' affinity for transparent risk-taking has magnified! Indeed, their cutting edge content has reached a larger audience. Imagine the pride and care our students take on their work as they prepare, record, and edit material that impacts their fellow students, community, and beyond. Thanks to podcasting, they've been gifted opportunities to present, blog, and teach other students and educators the essence of student-led projects.

Perhaps, my greatest joy with this passion project was on display at a recent podcast retreat that we put together this past spring. As our AWC students taught new wildcat podcasters, and enjoyed heartfelt video and live testimonials from listeners around the world, we ended our retreat with a surprise announcement for our students. CharacterStrong had agreed to be our official sponsor for the podcast. Watching the smiles, tears, and awe on our students' faces as they learned that they had impacted the very same people

(Norlin and Kraft) that originally inspired our student's work...JOY.

And perhaps, our best-kept secret of Award-Winning Culture is a brand built on bringing JOY to others!

Hans Appel, Counselor and Creator of "Award Winning Culture"
https://youtu.be/-vc7XE4J4Fs
Twitter: @HansNAppel
Podcast Episode #54: Create an Award-Winning Culture http://bit.
ly/episode54-hansappel

* * *

Build and Grow as an Influencer

If you believe in something that you think about all the time and fight for it, then you need to create a message around it. Many of the people on my podcast are authors. Most of them are educators who never thought they would be an author or a podcast host. Something changed in their lives. I've known Adam Welcome for years and have worked with his teachers when he was an assistant principal. He wrote a vignette about changing his WHY around his passion, running, in Chapter 8. He co-authored *Kids Deserve It* and *Run Like a Pirate*. Now he's the author of three books and definitely an influencer. When I asked Adam to write his WHY, he came up with the right story for this chapter.

* * *

Spreading Your Message
by Adam Welcome

I'm asked many questions from people on social media every week, and as I travel the country working and speaking with educators, even more questions in person. But the one question that comes up more than any other surprised me at first and really made me reflect on the path that has brought me to where I currently am.

What is it like to write a book?

Over and over for years, this question has come up, and at first, I'm sure there was a polite response I gave—saying how fortunate I am to be an author, the ability to spread my message, etc., etc. That first response didn't last long, because very quickly, I thought about my path and journey to writing a book.

Many people think it's an overnight success. Let me tell you that it's not.

If you want to write a book, here's my advice:
You have an idea.
Or maybe you've been doing something at your school or district that has been going well.
Curriculum is your passion, and you want to share your approach and what you've learned.
And sometimes, people I talk with have absolutely no idea what they want to write about, they just want to write a book.

The vast majority of times when I talk with people, I tell them the same exact thing.

Forget about writing a book.

Now I know this may sound contradictory as I've written three books myself, but I'm completely serious.

What I think people should focus on instead is just getting their message out, and then maybe a book becomes a part of the plan down the road.

If you have an idea or something you want to share, you need to be blogging about that idea on a weekly basis. I recommend people blog two to three times per week because it's a really great writing exercise and also serves many purposes.

When you blog about your idea consistently, you're building your audience. You're gathering readers that someday may potentially turn into people who will purchase your book. You may also realize that your idea really isn't a book; it's maybe just a few blog posts, and that's all you have for the idea.

But you won't figure that out unless you blog—that part is key.

What blogging regularly also does is help you to really sharpen your ideas. The more you write about a topic, the more you're going to think about that topic regularly. If you're writing, and thinking, then you're refining and analyzing and siphoning off all the 'extra' that doesn't need to be included in your message.

You're also finding out what resonates with other educators from around the world. You may think your idea is an absolute blockbuster, and using a blog to 'test' the market for your book idea is way easier and faster and cheaper than putting it into a book and then seeing what lands with the reader.

Another idea, instead of blogging, is to start a podcast. Podcasting was way ahead of its time ten years ago and has really found a resurgence in the last three to five years.

It's ridiculously easy to start a podcast and publish your

content from pretty much any platform you have. Maybe you think you don't have any time to blog. Well, you can record a podcast from your phone, in your car, while you're sitting in your driveway, or down the street from your house before you get home. The simplicity of it all is amazing and just another great way to publish and share your idea.

Make sure you're active on social media and building your network through Twitter chats, Voxer groups, and with other job-a-like educators. The vast majority of educators market and promote their books through Twitter. If you only Tweet every couple of weeks and haven't really invested in building out that network, I really think you're going to be at a disadvantage when your book does come out, and you're trying to build momentum around your ideas.

I was talking to someone the other day, and they were asking how I had so many followers on Twitter (which is actually not many compared to some), and the simple answer is that I put in the work and spend lots of time on the platform. When I don't spend time, it shows. But when I do, I see the difference in a major way, and it makes all that work totally worth it.

The last piece of advice before you approach a publisher—be patient. When I tell people that I've been blogging for over ten years, and started speaking for free years and years ago as well, they don't always believe it. There is no such thing as an overnight success. It's hard work, that is consistent and focused for years and years, period.

I guess the spoiler is I'm not really helping you get a book published, because there is lots of work to do before that happens. How passionate are you about your idea? Do you have the necessary experience to write and share it with the world?

Writing and publishing a book is absolutely amazing, but there are many other ways to share your passion and knowledge with the world! Good luck and share, share, share.

Adam Welcome, author, speaker, principal
Twitter: @mradamwelcome @kidsdeserveit

Episode #5 Podcast: Running Because Kids Deserve It https://barbarabray.net/2017/08/02/running-because-kids-deserve-it-with-adam-welcome/

Email: adamwelcome@gmail.com
Website: https://mradamwelcome.com/

———

Blogs: Adam Welcome: Life as a Digital Dad http://adamwelcome.blogspot.com/
Kids Deserve It http://www.kidsdeserveit.com/
Book: Welcome, A. (2019) Running Like a Pirate. San Diego, CA. Dave Burgess Consulting.

* * *

Elevator Speech

An elevator speech is like a startup pitch. It is about capturing the interest and imagination of someone you have just met—in about the time it might take both of you to enter an elevator and travel down to the lobby level.

Mark Wiskup, author of *The It Factor: Be the One People Like, Listen to, and Remember* (Wiskup, 2007), wrote why elevator pitches are important: *"Great communicators, those who connect quickly and strongly with others all the time, know how to communicate the essence of their message--succinctly and in a memorable way--whether or not there's an elevator in sight."*

Effective elevator pitches, writes Wiskup, are *"memorable, vivid, and unique to your voice and the way you talk."*

Elevator speeches are usually around 60 seconds and 100 words. I wrote my elevator speech for this book:

Do you ever feel like you are going through the motions to just get through the day? Do you continue to do what you do because you have always done it that way? You may not even have considered that you can change YOU and have more joyful experiences, but you can. When you know your WHY through your stories about YOU, and you have the strategies you need to believe in yourself, you will discover a more meaningful and purposeful life. Don't rent someone else's story. Read Define Your WHY so you can own your story and tell it.

Elevator speeches can be about your personal story and be what is driving your WHY. Shelly Vohra shared her WHY story in Chapter 6 about "Sharing Her Story to Inspire Others to Share Theirs." See how Shelly took the main points and turned it into an elevator pitch for her WHY.

* * *

My WHY (Elevator Speech)
by Shelly Vohra, Ed.D.

We live in a time where issues related to equity, inclusion, and diversity have never been more important. I grew up in a time where there were not many South Asians in my class. I could count on one hand how many racialized girls were in my school. My teachers were all white, whether male or female. Although I did well in school and was often considered the teachers' pet, I felt like they did not truly understand me, my culture, beliefs, and values. Now, our student body is comprised of kids from a variety of backgrounds who are seeking to be understood and valued. We need to ensure they feel represented in the teaching and learning happening in our classrooms. I feel it is important to share my story, so others feel like it is okay to share theirs — their highs, lows, struggles, and dreams.

Twitter: @raspberryberret3
Podcast Episode #3: https://barbarabray.net/2017/06/23/my-journey-into-inquiry/

* * *

Activity: Write your Elevator Speech for Your WHY

Elevator speeches or pitches need to be concise and capture your audience in the first 7-10 seconds, even if it is an audience of one person. Use these five steps and then write your speech (around 100 words) in your journal.

1. **Goal:** What is the goal for your pitch? You can start with a statement or a question about a problem to grab the audience. You may want to identify a problem that your audience has and how your WHY can be the solution.
2. **Solution:** What is your solution that you identified in #1? Explain how your WHY solves a problem.
3. **Making a Difference:** Why is your solution or idea better than other ideas? Why does your WHY make a difference?
4. **Ask to Believe:** Ask your audience a question or come up with a way to get them thinking that they can believe in your WHY or want to learn more about your WHY.
5. **Practice:** Go over your speech and edit it until you get your speech to 100 words. Practice it over and over until it sounds natural and not like you are reading it.

Questions to Ponder

- What are your hopes and dreams?
- Why is it important for you to write your Personal Bill of Rights?
- How do you feel about branding yourself and your WHY?
- What do you need to move forward to promote yourself and your WHY?

Wonderings

As an educator, I used to feel it was wrong to promote myself. I needed to focus on the kids, not me. But when I saw kids, young kids, feeling bad about themselves, I realized I needed to change my thinking. There's a difference between bragging, promoting, and sharing. If you really believe in something and are passionate about it, wrapping your passion as a message that makes sense moves it forward. I realized when I started my podcast, I was modeling behavior for others. Educators reached out to me to ask how they could do something like that or have their students host a podcast. Another reason I wanted to change the idea for branding was when I heard teachers say, "I'm just a teacher." Ouch! Teachers are not "just" anything. They are our heroes and need to be valued. Teachers have the most difficult job, training our future. If every educator demonstrates their own value, then they can model that and teach it to students. Actually, everyone needs to be valued and share why they believe in themselves.

 Believe in yourself and others will believe in you."

— Robert Cheeke

* * *

If you are looking for additional resources and more about this chapter, go to:

- the book study questions, go to https://barbarabray.net
- digital resources, go to http://bit.ly/defineyourwhy-digital
- discussions on Twitter, use the hashtag #defineyourWHY

WHY FIND PEOPLE WHO BELIEVE IN YOU?

> *Alone, we can do so little: Together, we can do so much."*
>
> — HELEN KELLER

Personal Learning Network

A Personal Learning Network (PLN) is an informal group of peers, colleagues, mentors, and professionals that you connect with to enhance your learning and take charge of your own professional learning. A PLN is a way of describing the group of people that you connect with to learn their ideas, their questions, their reflections, and their references.

Using Twitter

I started Twitter as soon as it opened, and then someone hacked my account in 2007. I wasn't sure what to do. I made a new account with the handle @bbray27. I let the few people I was connected with know that my old account was hacked and gave them my new handle. I didn't have that many followers or even really know the power of Twitter then. I thought the idea of writing 140 characters would be easy for me, but it was tough. I didn't realize how the connections I would make over the next 12+ years would help me become a better ME. Really, it did! I've met the most amazing people from around the world on Twitter. I learned tips about using Twitter from David Truss @datruss, who was one of the first people I followed when I started again with my new handle. Dave wrote a book on how to use Twitter for educators. I read it and loved it. I reached out to him to write about his WHY. Right away, I received a reply.

* * *

My WHY: Why Choose to be on Twitter
By David Truss

I started using Twitter in November of 2007. I jumped in rather unenthusiastically. Why the lack of enthusiasm? Because at the time, I wasn't updating my status regularly on Facebook, and I thought to myself, *"Why would I use a tool that only did one part of what Facebook did, when I already don't use that part of Facebook?"* However, I was blogging regularly, and several educational bloggers that I admired were blogging over and over again about 'the power of Twitter.' So, while November of 2007 may make me seem like an early adopter to you, I was dragged in late, in comparison to my blogging friends.

David Truss
@datruss

I'm twittering for the very first time. What is the most valuable aspect of this online experience for you?

12:33 AM · Nov 16, 2007 ·

What happened next was amazing. Suddenly I found that

some very interesting people were sharing resources that I would never have found had I not been on Twitter.

I use Twitter as a tool to connect and learn with, and from, other educators and social learners. No matter what field you are in, or what interests you are passionate to learn more about, you can use Twitter as a tool to connect and learn like I do. Twitter is a tool that I use continually, and as such, it has an advantage over conferences and one-off professional development (training) events... it's an amazing tool, and I maximize what I use it for, both professionally and personally.

If you think Twitter is 'dumb' or 'a waste of time,' well, then it will be. The hardest part of Twitter is that it does not have a friendly entry point. Until you develop a network, it actually takes a bit of work to make it meaningful and rewarding. Payoff comes when your network becomes better and more effective than Google when you connect with people that you actually categorize as valued friends (even if you've never met them face-to-face), and when your network starts to streamline the flow of information we are bombarded with, by selectively sharing only the best the web has to offer.

Since getting started can be one of the hardest things you do, finding someone to meet face-to-face to share how they use Twitter can be a powerful way to engage and learn. Find a face-to-face mentor, and don't be afraid to ask what you think might be dumb questions. Face-to-face meetings enrich your twitter relationship, and your twitter relationships enrich your experiences when you finally meet Twitter friends face-to-face. Remember, Twitter is a social media tool! Find a mentor and build a learning relationship to help you get going.

Here is another 'friendly entry point,' visit http://DavidTruss.com/TwitterEDU and pick up a free copy of *Twitter EDU*.

After this short read, you will be set up and ready to start or to enhance your journey as a networked educator.

Twitter: @datruss
LinkedIn: http://www.linkedin.com/in/davidtruss
Website: http://pairadimes.davidtruss.com/
Podcast: http://podcasts.davidtruss.com
Episode #34: Dream - Create - Learn
https://barbarabray.net/2018/03/06/dream-create-and-learn-with-dave-truss/

* * *

Why Twitter Chats?

A Twitter chat is a virtual meeting or gathering of people on Twitter to discuss a common topic. I'm constantly learning from the people who participate in Twitter chats. I remember the first chat that I jumped into, #edchat, and lurked in the background. I watched and learned. I realized that this is professional learning. I am learning in real-time from people all around the world. Here is a shortlist of several chats I suggest you check out (Conversion Chart - Pacific Time listed. MT +1, CT +2, ET +3, HST -3):

Sundays:

3:00 am	#TLAPDownUnder	weekly
3:30 am	#aussieED	weekly
5:30 am	#HackLearning	weekly
4:00 pm	#GratefulEdu	Every other week
4:30 pm	#BookCampPD	weekly
	#TeachPos	weekly
5:00 pm	#ecet2	weekly
6:00 pm	#BuildHOPEedu	weekly
	#PrinLeaderChat	weekly
	#ALTEdChat	weekly

Mondays:

4:00 pm	#rethink_learning (I'm co-host)	Every other week
4:30 pm	#FormativeChat	weekly
	#EdTechChat	weekly
5:00 pm	#LearnLAP	weekly
	#NYEDChat	weekly
	#WonderChat	1st Monday
6:00 pm	#TLAP	weekly
7:00 pm	#ResilienceChat	weekly

Tuesdays:

4:00 pm	#2PencilChat	weekly
	#EdChat	weekly
5:00 pm	#PBLchat	weekly
6:22 pm	#822chat	weekly
6:30 pm	#TeacherMyth	weekly

Wednesdays:

5:00 pm	#SuptChat	1st Wednesday
5:30 pm	#CorwinTalks	3rd Wednesday
	#KidsDeserveIT	weekly
6:00 pm	#CelebratED	weekly

Thursdays:

12:00 pm	#Ukedchat	weekly
3:00 pm	#FutureOfSchool	Last Thursday
4:00 pm	#WhatIsSChool	weekly
5:00 pm	#MasteryChat	weekly

Fridays:

4:00 pm	#WolfPackEdu	weekly
4:30 pm	#TeachMindful	Every other week
	#StuCenterClass	Every other week

Saturdays:

5:00 am	#satchat	weekly
6:00 am	#EduGladiators	weekly
6:30 am	#LeadUpChat	weekly
7:00 am	#CrazyPLN	weekly
7:30 am	#LeadLap	weekly

I want to give a shoutout to #EduMatch Tweet & Talk Panel on Sundays at 6 pm ET that you can sign up to participate at http://podcasts.edumatch.org/tweettalk. Check the hashtag #educhatlist for more or go to https://sites.google.com/site/twittereducationchats/education-chat-official-list

If you would like to host your own Twitter chat, go to *How to Host a Twitter Chat* at http://rite.ly/wjEY

Social Media Apps

Pinterest (www.pinterest.com)

According to Meng (2019), Pinterest is a social network that allows users to visually share and discover new interests by posting (known as 'pinning' on Pinterest) images or videos to their own or others' boards (i.e., a collection of 'pins,' usually with a common theme) and browsing what other users have pinned. You can perform standard social networking functions such as following the boards of your friends, liking and commenting on other users' pins, re-pinning content to their own boards, sharing others' pins on Facebook and Twitter, or via email, and even embedding individual pins on your website or blog. How could Pinterest support you and your WHY?

1. Set up an account and add your picture and a board cover to your profile.
2. Use the board's description to insert keywords and hashtags that connect to you.
3. Make sure your images on your website or on Pinterest are optimized as landscape and scaled at 600-pixel width with an aspect ratio of either 2:3 or 1:3.5.
4. Add your logo to the bottom of all your images to boost your WHY.
5. Actively pin to your board, but space out your pins. You can use Pinterest's analytics to keep track of your activity.

Instagram (www.instagram.com)

There are many different social media platforms out there. Why use Instagram? Instagram is considered to be the best social media platform for engagement or your ability as a brand to connect with your followers. It's visual, simple, and emphasizes photos more than any other social media platform. You can strengthen your social media presence and promote your WHY. You can even build relationships with influencers and build brand awareness around YOU. Check out Instagram Stories to share your WHY. How can Instagram support your WHY?

1. At the top of your page, you'll see a series of photos or videos.
2. This is a way to share "moments" of your day quickly and easily.
3. Everything that you put together for your Story becomes a slideshow on Instagram.
4. This stays on your account for twenty-four hours and then disappears.

5. Add another element to your Story, and you're bumped to
   the front of the line.

Voxer (www.voxer.com)

According to Birdsong (2017), Voxer allows a user to send a real-time
voice message (like a walkie-talkie) to another Voxer user. Users can
also leave Voxer messages much like a voicemail. The app sends your
voice in near-real-time to the person you reach out to. They can listen
to your message when it is convenient for them. You can touch a field
to type out text if you want, and there's a camera button if you want to
take a picture to send, or you can pick one from your library (Parker,
2014). All your messages are shown in a standard text message list
view. You also can listen to previous audio messages by touching
them. How might you use Voxer to support your WHY?

1. Touch a large button at the bottom to start speaking, and let
   go when you're done. You can set Voxer up to click start, and
   then when finished, click again to end the voiceover.
2. Set up large group chats or teams to send messages to
   everyone at once.
3. See a written copy of audio messages instead of listening to
   them.
4. Recall and delete any unwanted messages you have sent.
   {Paid account only}
5. Have access to your entire message history.

Other Social Media to promote your WHY

I use *Facebook* for personal connections, sharing photos, stories, and
videos. I set up a Facebook page for Rethinking Learning (Rethink-
ingLearning) to promote posts, podcasts, events, resources, articles,
and more. You, too, can have a separate page for your WHY or a book
or something else you want to promote.

LinkedIn is the best for me to promote my work and connect to others outside of Twitter. I use LinkedIn for my personal and professional accounts. I found that using my name as my brand on LinkedIn is the best way for me to connect with other educators.

YouTube is a great way to learn about most anything. It is also where you can share short videos promoting your WHY. After you create your elevator pitch, how about creating a video with your phone to share your pitch? Simple. Turn your phone sideways and use your webcam with a video recorder like QuickTime player. Practice and then create your video. Share it by uploading it to YouTube. You can even embed it on your blog or website.

 Social media shouldn't just be a part of the conversation, it can be a part of the solution; not just because of the potential of widespread messaging, but because when students actually create using technology and social media, they are learning about the interplay of text, production, and audience which will serve to help them become critical of the media they consume."

— Julie Andsager, PhD. (Casa-Todd, 2017, p. 79)

Sharing your WHY

When you share your WHY, you are modeling leadership. I read Jennifer Casa-Todd's book, *Social LEADia* and learned so much about using, modeling, and teaching social media After having a conversation with Jennifer for Episode #59 for my podcast, I decided to read her book again. When I started writing this chapter, I wanted to take what I shared about creating a brand as a professional to student learning and digital leadership. I reached out to Jennifer to have her write a vignette, and I learned more about modeling digital leadership from her story.

* * *

Engaging and Modeling Digital Leadership
By Jennifer Casa-Todd

When I joined Twitter in 2011 and realized that many people were like-minded and supportive and generous with their resources and ideas, it was completely transformational. I tried to get everyone I knew on Twitter. But in my role as Literacy Consultant, I had to be mindful that not everyone benefits from a one-size-fits-all way to learn. Just like our students, for some teachers, Twitter just didn't jive. This was in and around the same time, I discovered Voxer.

I was first introduced to the EduMatch (@Edu_Match) Voxer group created by Sarah Thomas (@sarahdateechur) in 2015. Voxer is literally a walkie-talkie app that allows participants to talk in real-time (if people are online at the same time) and send a text, picture, or video. Messages, not listened to in real-time, are stored on your device and can be listened to when you are in your car, getting ready for your day, or instead of watching reruns on television. What I love about Voxer is that it really allows for more intimate community building than Twitter, LinkedIn, or Facebook. This is because there are no character limits, but especially because when you hear someone's voice and intonation as they speak, squeal, laugh, or cry, even though you've never met this person face-to-face, you feel as if you really know them. One of the most fascinating aspects of this group is its diversity. During one chat session, we learned that people in EduMatch were of different faiths: Buddhist, Muslim, Catholic, Jewish, Lutheran, Mormon, and Presbyterian. It was really neat to know that despite our very different religious backgrounds, our common interest in education, and meeting the needs of our learners trumped anything else, but more importantly for me is the ability to hear many diverse voices which may be missing from my own geographical environment. This is what I want my students to experience positively.

Over the years, I have joined a variety of Voxer groups and within the last two years, a personal group which we have called, #My53s. This group isn't particularly aimed at educational sharing or problem-solving (although we also do share our challenges regarding EDU). It is a platform for friendship, and it is amazing to me to live in a world where I can find a space where I am not the "lone wolf." In my OGC (Our Global Classroom) Voxer group, we combine goofiness with our common goal of connecting classrooms to each other and the world.

I make time for Voxer on my way to school and back because I value the relationships which have developed there, but in the past few years, I have also come to appreciate the diversity of platforms that can support my learning and growth as well. I have followed many educators on Snapchat and am a part of a Sing-off group where we sing to one another (not well), and laugh and relish in being goofy! It has been a great way to explore the many features of Snapchat. My Facebook group for *Social LEADia* and the various groups I have joined, which are geared towards Teacher-Librarians, or Breakout EDU, for example, give me access to the ideas of educators who are not on Twitter, in a platform not limited to 280 characters. And on Instagram, which is very visual, I get insight into the classrooms and libraries of others and have gotten so many ideas. It is also where I get to know people in my PLN on a more personal level. For me, technology and social media connect me to other human beings whose perspective I could never get otherwise.

"Social media is social currency for young people."

One quote I share in Social LEADia is that connected learners need connected leaders and teachers. It is hard to ask the right questions and guide and mentor kids around a healthy and positive relationship with technology if we are not familiar with the tools our kids are using. More importantly for me is engaging and modeling digital leadership: learning and sharing learning, empowering and celebrating others, and making a positive difference. This is my WHY. I don't think we should teach kids how to brand themselves, and I believe that what we share and how we share it are really important. I am not concerned with how many followers I have; I use my device and social media for digital leadership. In my work with students, and in my research, I have learned that many students don't necessarily know any other way to use their devices and/or social media. In my experience, when you show students how to use social media to learn and to form meaningful connections, then that is what you will see. If we don't show kids anything different, we won't see them act differently.

Jennifer Casa-Todd, Teacher-Librarian and author
Websites: https://jcasatodd.com, https://www.socialleadia.org/
Twitter: @JCasaTodd #socialleadia
Facebook: https://www.facebook.com/socialLEADia/
Episode #59: Moving Students from Digital Citizenship to Digital Leadership
http://bit.ly/episode59-casatodd
Book: Casa-Todd, J. (2017) Social LEADia. San Diego, CA: Dave Burgess Consulting.

* * *

Face-to-Face Meetings and Conferences

There is nothing like meeting people face-to-face that you know online. I always look forward to having conversations and spending time to get to know people in my PLN better. I started going to the CUE conference in 1992. It wasn't long before I started recognizing the same people at different conferences. We became family. My first ISTE conference (International Society for Technology in Education) was in 1997. I didn't know anyone, but everyone was open and friendly. Many educators I met then I'm still friends with today. I recommend educators to attend at least one conference each year. The connections you make at the conference can open doors for you to help you on your journey.

HackEd is an unconference the day before ISTE, and I found the discussions were open-ended where everyone had the opportunities to lead. There are multiple ways to join in unconferences, such as EdCamps, CoffeeEdu, Teachmeets, and Tweet and Talks. All of these are open-ended meetings, face-to-face, and online. The first time I was involved in an unconference, I didn't know the procedures and was a little confused. Someone came up to me and helped me. All I had to do was to put a check on the topics on flipcharts that I was interested in. Those with the most checks then were scheduled during the day. Everyone had a voice in the vote. Then everyone had a voice to participate or even leave and go to another session.

Activities to Build Your PLN

1- Add and Share Conferences, Twitter Chats, and More

I realize after reading what I have in this chapter that I am missing many other ways to connect, share, and learn.

- Go to http://bit.do/defineyourwhy-digital to add any
  conferences (with links), EdCamps (with pictures/dates),

Twitter chats (with date, time, hashtag), and any other opportunities for others to connect.
- Add any reflections of any conferences or other experiences in your journal that help you connect and learn.

Questions to Ponder

- What do you do to build your network?
- What is the best platform for you to connect online?
- Do you regularly attend a conference or meeting? How does it help you grow?
- What goals do you have to build and grow your personal learning network?

2- Plan How You Can Build Your PLN

My passion was to make a difference in education and guide educators to empower student agency. My goal was to share other people's stories. So my plan was to look for stories and why they matter. I needed to know my story and realized that some of my personal stories impacted my professional life. I reached out to thought leaders and inspirational educators for their stories on Twitter and through other connections using hashtags around agency, hope, positivity, personalized learning, and more. My ultimate goal was to become a storyteller and be a better speaker to share stories that touch people's hearts.

No matter where you are with connecting to others in your profession or around your passion, you can start or grow your PLN with people with similar interests. Review the above Questions to Ponder before starting your plan.

- Define your goal(s) to build your PLN. You may find that you have different personal and professional goals.
- After you figured out your WHY, you may have some

questions about determining your goal. What would you like
to learn or change about you?

- How can this goal work for your professional and/or
  personal life?
- Based on the goal for your WHY, develop steps to meet that
  goal. Find and follow Twitter hashtags that are similar to
  your WHY.
- Based on your goal, determine the tags, keywords, and
  hashtags you can use to find and follow others. In Twitter,
  you can search for people with a hashtag.
- Identify the best platforms to join or conferences to attend to
  connect with people with similar interests.
- Write in your journal about the growth of your PLN. Start a
  blog or write about your WHY on another site like Medium
  to reflect on building your PLN.

I never knew that I would be able to connect with people around the
world through social media like I did. The power of the connections I
made have grown into deep friendships. I am grateful for the people
I've met and learned from. I hope you build and grow your PLN to
meet people that can help you define your WHY.

Wonderings

If you are a teacher or administrator and would like to connect with
other educators, there are many opportunities now to do that.
Starting with social media, you can dip your toes into Twitter and
follow people to test the water. Go to an EdCamp and participate in
some of the discussions. If you are an administrator, there are Twitter
chats and conferences for you. I know parents and school board
members who are interested in what is going in education will learn
more by going to education events. You are welcome to join in also.
Maybe I'll see you online or at a conference. When I decided to start
my podcast, I was part of a network of educators who had inspired
me. I reached out and asked if they would like to be on my podcast.

The conversations were easy for me because many of the educators I know are connectors and storytellers. You never know where the connections you make will take you.

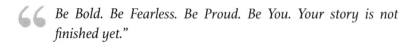 *Be Bold. Be Fearless. Be Proud. Be You. Your story is not finished yet."*

— Thomas C. Murray from his book, Personal and
Authentic (2019)

* * *

If you are looking for additional resources and more about this chapter, go to:

- the book study questions, go to https://barbarabray.net
- digital resources, go to http://bit.ly/defineyourwhy-digital
- discussions on Twitter, use the hashtag #defineyourWHY

WHY BE THE CHIEF STORYTELLER OF YOU AND YOUR WHY?

I am not a teacher, but an awakener."

— Robert Frost

Use your voice to share your story. This chapter will share examples of people who write and speak about being positive, kind, joyful, and passionate about their WHY as they spread their messages. I wanted to share different examples throughout this book and how defining our WHY can be about our struggles, possibly the pain we had, challenges that pushed us, and doors that were opened or closed. Telling your story your way helps guide you along your journey to define your WHY.

Why Your Voice and Your WHY Matters

When you know your WHY and live it, it is important for you to tell your story before someone else does. I mentioned throughout this book the idea of not renting someone else's story as your own. You are unique and have had different experiences than anyone else. No one is like you anywhere in the world. There may be someone who looks like you (or you are a twin), but your experiences, your connections, and your memories are all yours, and no one shares those. What happens to you impacts you and can change you if you are willing.

I've known Ken Shelton for almost 20 years. I am fortunate to have had great talks with Ken that pushed my thinking, especially around equity and diversity issues. I applaud him for not giving up on what he believes. Ken was a guest in one of my earlier podcasts: Episode #19 on Passion for Storytelling and Equity. When I heard Ken's powerful WHY speech at FlipGrid Live at the ISTE 2019 conference in Philadelphia, I asked him if he would share it. Lucky for me, he said YES!

* * *

Speaking Your Truth
by Ken Shelton

Ever wonder
Why some succeed
While others fail
Why so many factors determine your future
your access
Opportunity
Pre-determined
Pre-measured
Pre-colored. But not for my color

Why is success
dependent on the system
not independent of the system

How can I learn in a system

not set up for my success
but I digress

Sometimes my why
makes a tear run
Like a black teen
From the blunt force of a baton
Carried from generational scars
Originating from afar

I was only nine
When I was given the talk
Be careful son
Of the way you dress
You speak
You walk
Don't Run

Like a key that would unlock me
And break the cycle
A system that would rather roll over me
Than carry me

How can I succeed
in a system that would plot my incarceration
Instead of my education

My why is speaking my truth
I will no longer be a victim of the shackles of a foreign
    institution
My determination will free me from my mental subjugation

Speaking your truth is the thing you should do
speaking your truth is you being you

Therefore I will no longer deny
what's my why
because if your why is the truth
then I say why not

Check out Ken's video of his WHY at https://vimeo.com/348917098

Twitter: @k_shelton
Episode #19 Podcast: A Passion for Storytelling and Equity
https://barbarabray.net/2017/11/11/a-passion-for-storytelling-and-equity-with-ken-shelton/

Pinterest: http://pinterest.com/kenshelton/
Website: http://kennethshelton.net/
Ken's Photography site: http://www.kensheltonphoto.com/

* * *

 To live is the rarest thing in the world. Most people just exist."

— Oscar Wilde

WHY Your Passion Matters

I met Tamara Letter at the 2016 ISTE (International Society of Technology in Education) conference, where she was doing an inspiring poster session. She knew me and rushed over to hug me. I loved her energy and had to get to know her better. Everything about Tamara is joyful, caring, and giving. I followed her journey and invited her to cross-post Planning for Passion that she wrote to put on my website. (https://barbarabray.net/2017/04/22/planning-passion/). She shared Passion Project Display Boards, Kindness Journals, and a Kindness Fair. Right after her Kindness Fair, I had a conversation with Tamara for my new podcast. She was Episode #2: Passion Through Kindness, and I was lucky to review and write a testimonial for her amazing book, *Passion for Kindness* (Letter, 2019).

* * *

Discovering Your Life's Purpose: Plot Twist
By Tamara Letter, M.Ed.

When does one discover their life's purpose? At the age of twenty, I thought I had it all figured out. I was going to be a wife, a teacher, and a mom in that order. My purpose was pretty simple: do those three things, do them well, and life will be complete. Despite the challenges of childhood and some pretty tough bumps along the way, I knew this was my destiny, and I was content to focus on this path.

Two decades passed with the blink of an eye, and there I stood: A wife. A teacher. A mom. Purpose fulfilled, or so I thought. Then came the plot twist no one saw coming. My life's purpose had just begun.

It started with a kindness project for my 40th birthday. I decided to complete 40 acts of kindness and blog a story about each event. Through that journey, I developed an insatiable desire to make the world a better place. My filter on life and the lens from which I viewed others no longer had the smudges of negativity. I discovered the more I shared kindness with others, the more joyful I became, which spilled into every aspect of my life.

My perception didn't erase the hardships and oppression I saw around me; rather, I became more deliberate in my acknowledgment of those things I couldn't control. Instead of turning away or feeling powerless to change things beyond my reach, I embraced the mindset that small acts of kindness were still important, and, for some, could be life-changing.

I stretched myself beyond the thin lines of comfort and conformity, sharing conversations with strangers through social media platforms. I quickly discovered others who shared a passion for kindness, and together, we wrapped ourselves with purposeful positivity to get us through the toughest of days.

Since the start of that transformation, my mindset has melted the linear lines and revealed a circle of continuity. I am a wife. A teacher. A mom. But I am also a Kindness Cultivator, one who deliberately works for the greater good, sharing the experiences I learned about kindness with others. My passion is now my purpose, woven deeply in who I am, what I say, and how I share my life with others.

It's the unexpected plot twist that completely changed my life. It pushed me to become a better writer. It challenged me to become a published author. It guided me to shine with inspiration for others. Each day I deliberately scatter seeds of kindness to those around me, knowing that one day those seeds will take root, grow tall, then scatter seeds of their own.

Embrace your passions and allow them to take you to places unknown. Seek out those who will readily pour into your life just as you will pour into theirs. Allow yourself the opportunity to dream big and discover more. It's in that quest of passion that you may discover your purpose was there all along!

Tamara Letter, M.Ed.

Educator, Author, and Motivational Speaker
Mechanicsville, VA
Book Information: (Letter, 2019) http://bit.ly/DBCkindness
Email: celebratekindness@gmail.com
Website: www.tamaraletter.com
Twitter: @tamaraletter
Instagram: @tamaraletter
Episode #2 Passion Through Kindness https://barbarabray.net/
2017/06/06/passion-through-kindness/

* * *

 Practice random acts of kindness and senseless acts of beauty."

— ANNE HERBERT

Self-Advocate for Your Why

Do you believe in something so much that it is all you talk about? I know I've been there, and didn't realize I had turned people off. I was not explaining my ideas right. I realized you have to find a way to share your WHY and what you believe in a way that excites and inspires people. The idea of being an advocate for your WHY seemed foreign to me. That was way before I started my podcast. It wasn't long before I got caught up in their stories. I also learned that when they were able to do something about what they were passionate about, they did something about it. Many were educators who led the way by sharing how they transform teaching and learning. They shared examples on social media, at conferences, and wrote books.

I learned about Darren Ellwein on Twitter and met him in person at the TIES conference in December 2016, and later in California in 2017. He is the principal of South Harrisburg Middle School in

Harrisburg, South Dakota, where learning is personal and innovative. I'm fortunate to have had a conversation with him as Episode #29. I shared in Chapter 9 how his teachers empowered kids with the UN SDGs. He wanted to share all of the innovative practices with the world. Darren and Derek McCoy co-authored *The Revolution* to spark a revolution all about empowered learning. I asked Darren if he would share a short WHY it was necessary to spark a revolution.

* * *

We Need to Spark a Revolution
By Darren Ellwein

In 2019, I co-wrote *The Revolution* with Derek McCoy. We wanted to spark a revolution that revealed how empowered learning creates impactful results. Implementing this change is not the norm and can be met with resistance. I have lived through these tough times...and survived to see kids succeed in unique experiences. There is not much 'traditional' in our school in South Dakota.

From personalized learning to design thinking classes to our global connections, we want our kids to drive their learning and solve big problems. This kind of change is dependent on you taking risks and displaying persistence and grit when the water dumpers come to put out your fire. I recently told my staff that there is no ending point for us. Each year is a new iteration. Why? Think about the 'who' you receive each year. Each group of learners is unique and different each year. It is our job to serve them by meeting their unique needs. This is WHY each year should be a new iteration. This is WHY we need to learn how to empower kids to make decisions.

Twitter: @dellwein

Website: Under the Influence: https://edtransformed.wordpress.com/
Book: Ellwein, D & McCoy, D. (2019) The Revolution. San Diego,
CA: Dave Burgess Consulting, Inc.
Podcast: Episode#23 on Inspiring Kids to Greatness: https://
barbarabray.net/2017/12/06/inspiring-kids-to-greatness-with-
darren-ellwein/

＊ ＊ ＊

 When the world is silent, even one voice becomes powerful."

— MALALA YOUSAFZAI

Be Brave and Step Out of Your Comfort Zone

It is too easy to stay the same and not change. I went through a period where I was comfortable but not happy. I look back at my life and wonder why I continued doing dental hygiene when I loved teaching. I thought it was because I didn't want to let my patients down. After I left, they had a new hygienist and moved on without me. No one is indispensable. That hurt! I had put too much into building the practice and caring, but the next hygienist was caring and helped build the practice, maybe even better than I did. I'm saying this because I believed the wrong story. I didn't listen to my heart. I was doing a disservice to my patients because I didn't put my heart into my work.

I've heard from teachers who were struggling in their jobs. Several were telling me they didn't feel valued or listened to. Others had no time to think or catch their breath during the day. When I asked them if they had talked to their administrator, some were afraid to let them know how they felt. I asked some if they wanted to look for a different teaching job. Many told me that they wouldn't leave because of the kids. Sound familiar? The kids need you to be happy and not struggling. If you move to a new school, they have kids there that need you too. But no matter where you are, they need you to be strong, brave, and passionate about what you do.

> *Promise me to remember that you are braver than you believe, stronger than you seem, and smarter than you think."*

— A.A. MILNE

I shared in Chapter 7 on empathy how all of us have stress and may have a fear of failure. I wanted to bring that back because it just pulled everything together. When I have been talking with teachers face-to-face or in workshops and video conferences, I can hear their fear. I asked if their students were compliant or moving to self-directed. Everywhere I asked this, there were a large number of teachers that said that over 50% of the students were compliant. I was shocked. After working for over 30 years, it seemed to me like we were going backward. Why are our students compliant now? They know more because of the Internet, smartphones, and apps. It seemed like we were going backward because many teachers and others outside the profession learned how to be compliant. In fact, that's how they were taught. They told me that the system and too many initiatives didn't allow them to think out of the box or time to get to know their students. Whew!

I wrote this book for anyone who wants to define their WHY. Since I work with educators, I wanted to provide a way to advocate for teachers through their WHY. After I had these conversations about compliance, I thought it's about feeling powerless in their positions. I realized this is what can cause apathy and burnout. I reached out to a group of educators to let them know I'm here for them if they want a coach or someone to listen to their stories. I think that's what we can do for each other.

I adapted "The Comfort Zone" by @thewealthhike at www.

thewealthhike.com. The image starts on the left with the Comfort Zone. We may go back to the Comfort Zone when issues come up or the Fear Zone when we feel we are not heard, or something happens that triggers our fears. But it is how we handle those fears and feelings. I wanted you to see through this graphic that you can move to the Learning Zone about something you are excited about learning. I hope some of the activities in this book got you up and excited about trying something new.

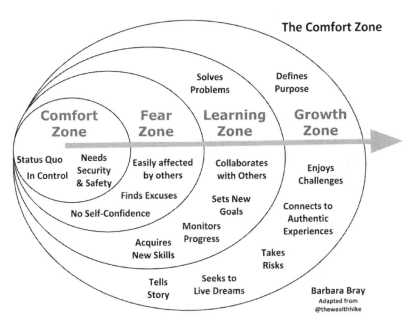

Fig. 12.1 The Comfort Zone adapted from www.thewealthhike.com

> *Don't be afraid to start over again. This time you're not starting from scratch, you're starting from experience."*
>
> — UNKNOWN

It is too easy to stay in the status quo and to believe that you cannot or will not change. Some have told me that they need security and safety first and won't change. This was my challenge. I wrote this book because many educators and some friends have told me that they wanted to give up. I needed to write this book for those teachers, administrators, or good friends who were losing hope. If this is you, I hope at least one or more of the ideas or activities get you thinking that you do have the power to change or make a different choice. Every day, we are subjected to things that happen to us. Everything that happens changes our brain. It becomes a memory and affects what we may do next. Guess what? **That is learning.** Every experience can be a lesson and a blesson. A BLESSON.

 My new word: BLESSON. It's when you're able to view painful lessons as blessons. In other words...a Blesson is what happens when you see the blessing in the lesson that your challenge taught you."

— KAREN SALMANSOHN

We can stay afraid and not believe in ourselves, but we still ARE learning. Everyday. Every experience is changing you. The concern I have is if you don't take a role in how and what you learn, you will be living the wrong story. Just like I did. If you don't know your WHY and continue down a road without purpose, you'll be living a life that you don't have any control over. You may be following what someone else tells you to do.

Think about your life. Do you feel you are living in fear and finding excuses to move ahead? Have you ever asked WHY you are here, and what is your purpose? Since you made it to this last chapter, you probably have asked yourself a few of the questions that I proposed to you throughout this book. Keep asking. Keep discovering more about you. You are worth it!!

 I am still learning."

— MICHELANGELO AT AGE 87

A Few More Questions to Ponder

- Where are you in the Comfort Zone? Are you in different zones with different things happening in your life?
- Are you ready to change? Is anything keeping you from changing?
- Do you have a time in your past that you realized that you were the only person you could change?
- Why is it important for you to define your WHY? Why do you need to learn and live on purpose?

You as Your Chief Storyteller

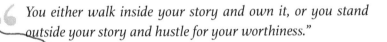

You either walk inside your story and own it, or you stand outside your story and hustle for your worthiness."

— Brené Brown

You have a story. I know you do. When you tell your story your way, you will be heard. It is scary to open up and share your stories. I know. I had trouble at first because I wasn't sure how others would understand me and what I was saying. When I went through what I shared in this book for me, I learned that I just had to take a chance and some risks, because I believed in something. I did. I believed that it was time to shake everything up in education. I had been sharing WHY our kids needed to own the learning. I heard it from others and shared their beliefs. But my voice was not enough. I shared other people's stories through my blogs and invited many to write guest blogs. All of this was before all the amazing tools and social media were available.

When I wrote the professional development column for CUE, I reached out to educators who told me amazing stories about innovation happening in their classrooms. That's when I got it. I just have to ask people to tell their stories. I needed to encourage them to share. It was tough pulling those stories out of some teachers. There were a few who just didn't believe in themselves enough or that they didn't think their stories were that unique. But they were, and they are. Then with my podcast, I found that there was power in the stories they shared with me. I love the conversations and plan on continuing with a new direction around Define Your WHY. I am grateful to the people who shared their stories throughout this book. All I did was ask them. They put their hearts out there, sharing memories and a piece of their lives. It took me some time to get it that our WHY is made up of all the stories and experiences in our lives. Then I realized I wasn't living my story. I was renting other people's stories. People who thought they were helping me, but actually, I made a choice that I didn't have a voice in my journey. Now I do. I wrote this quote and am planning my Ted Talk using this as my throughline:

Don't RENT someone else's story, OWN your story and TELL It.

Your stories make you who you are. You have stories to tell. If you don't tell your stories, who will? It's your time now. You have those stories, and they are all about YOU and your WHY.

I want you to think about a few of the activities you did through this book. Which ones stood out? You can go back and do any of them again. Take out your journal and see what you wrote.

Think about your backstory you wrote. What stood out? How did you feel? Can you weave in your stories with your experiences and why those support your WHY?

Go back to your journal again and again. Read and review what you wrote. Add to it. Several people who did this mentioned that they ended up having different journals. One for reflections and the other for activities.

Consider all the stories people added to my book to define their

WHY. All I did was ask them if they would write a story for my book. I asked people to be on my podcast. Don't be afraid to ask. You will be surprised who will respond and say YES.

Remember the draft WHY statement that you wrote. Go ahead and review it and, if you want to, update it.

Your WHY statement:

To _____ *[contribution]*
so that _____ *[impact]*.

Let's review what you came up with for your *ikigai*. Is this your WHY? Now that you made it to the last chapter, has your WHY changed? Were you able to brainstorm and prioritize your passions as your WHY? Maybe you wrote your Personal Beliefs and your elevator speech. Wow! After I did that, I was empowered to want to do more and learn more about my WHY. I hope you do that.

What you explored through this book was to discover the real YOU. Keep working on your story, and your WHY will grow. Your WHY may change throughout your life, along with your stories. Those stories will inspire you to grow and want to learn more. Each time you share your story, it will make you stronger.

 Go with your Strengths and Develop Your Passion through Your Stories to Discover Your WHY."

— Barbara Bray

* * *

If you are looking for additional resources and more about this chapter, go to:

- the book study questions, go to https://barbarabray.net
- digital resources, go to http://bit.ly/defineyourwhy-digital
- discussions on Twitter, use the hashtag #defineyourWHY

YOUR WHY AND YOUR CALL TO ACTION

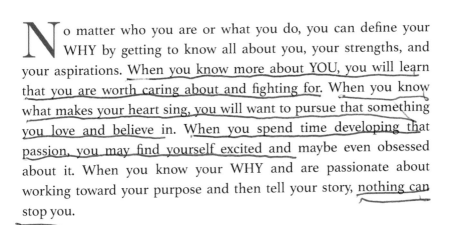

No matter who you are or what you do, you can define your WHY by getting to know all about you, your strengths, and your aspirations. When you know more about YOU, you will learn that you are worth caring about and fighting for. When you know what makes your heart sing, you will want to pursue that something you love and believe in. When you spend time developing that passion, you may find yourself excited and maybe even obsessed about it. When you know your WHY and are passionate about working toward your purpose and then tell your story, nothing can stop you.

REFERENCES

Blackstock, C. (2017, November 21). The Emergence of the Breath of Life Theory. Retrieved September 29, 2019, from Indigenous Language Learning at indigenouslanguagelearning.ca/teacher/graduate/the-emergence-of-the-breath-of-life-theory

Bray, B., & McClaskey, K. (2015). *Make Learning Personal: The what, who, wow, where, and why.* Thousand Oaks, CA: Corwin.

Bray, B., & McClaskey, K. (2017). *How to Personalize Learning: A practical guide for getting started and going deeper.* Thousand Oaks, CA: Corwin.

Brown, B. (2012, September 11). *Daring Greatly: How the courage to be vulnerable transforms the way we live, love, parent, and lead.* New York, NY: Avery.

Brown, B. (2018). *Dare to Lead: Brave work, tough conversations, whole hearts.* New York, NY: Random House.

Cantrell, G. (2018). Data Science is the Lifeblood of the Digital Economy. Retrieved September 29, 2019, from https://www.jabil.com/insights/blog-main/data-science-the-lifeblood-of-the-digital-economy.html

Casa-Todd, J. (2017). *Social LEADia: Moving students from digital citizenship to digital leadership*. San Diego, CA: Dave Burgess Consulting, Inc.

Couros, G. (2015). *The Innovator's Mindset: Empower learning, unleash talent, and lead a culture of creativity*. San Diego, CA: Dave Burgess Consulting, Inc.

Csíkszentmihályi, M. (1996). *Creativity: Flow and the psychology of invention and discover*. New York, NY: Harper Collins Publishers.

Dene Poth, R. (2019, July 15). *The Future Is Now: Looking back to move ahead*. Nashville, TN: EduGladiators LLC.

Duckworth, S. (2019, February 13). *How to Sketchnote: A step-by-step manual for teachers and students*. Online Publishing: ElevateBooksEdu.

Dweck, C. (2007, December 26). *Mindset: New psychology of success*. New York, NY: Penguin Random House.

Ellwein, D., & McCoy, D. (2019). *The Revolution: It's time to empower change in our schools*. San Diego, CA: Dave Burgess Consulting, Inc.

Emerich France, P. (2019). *Reclaiming Personalized Learning A pedagogy for restoring equity and humanity in our classrooms*. Thousand Oaks, CA: Corwin.

Froehlich, M. (2018). *The Fire Within: Lessons from defeat that have ignited a passion for learning* . Alexandria, VA: EduMatch.

Frontier, T., & Rickabaugh, J. (2014). *Five Levers to Improve Learning: How to prioritize for powerful results in your school.* Alexandria, VA: ASCD.

Gerstein, J. (2019) *Learning in the Making: How to plan, execute, and assess makerspace lessons. Alexandria,* VA: ASCD.

Gruener, B. (2014) *What's Under Your Cape: superheroes of the character kind.* Northville, MI: Ferne Press.

Gill, B. (2017). *Discover your Passion or ikigai with 4 Simple Tips.* Retrieved August 14, 2019 from https://www.forbes.com/sites/bhaligill/2017/09/29/discover-your-passion-or-ikigai-with-4-simple-tips/#259d6fa753f7

Heavy Head, R. (2007, December 17). Rediscovering Blackfoot Science: How First Nations Helped Develop a Keystone of Modern Psychology. Retrieved September 21, 2019, from http://www.sshrc-crsh.gc.ca/society-societe/stories-histoires/story-histoire-eng.aspx?story_id=91

Humphries, M. (2019, 19). A Movement to Transform West Virginia Coal Miners into Beekeepers is Great for the Planet. Retrieved October 2, 2019, from http://nationswell.com/west-virginia-coal-alternative-beefarming/

Johnson, S. (2018, September 20). The Blackfoot/Maslow connection. Retrieved August 14, 2019, from https://sa-exchange.ca/the-blackfoot-maslow-connection/

Letchford, L. (2018) *Reversed: A memoir.* 1st Edition. Irvine, CA: Acorn.

Letter, T. (2019, February 14). *A Passion for Kindness: Making the world a better place to lead, love, and learn.* San Diego, CA: Dave Burgess Consulting, Inc.

Markham, B. (1983). *West with the Night.* New York, NY: North Point Press.

Martin-Kniep, G. (2012). Neuroscience of engagement and SCARF: why they matter to school. Retrieved September 4, 2019, from https://lciltd.org/WebsitePublications/HandbookNeuroleadership_EngagementArticleGMK.pdf

Maslow, A. (1943). A Theory of Human Motivation. Retrieved September 29,2019, from Psychological Review, 50(4), 370-96

McLeod, S. A. (2018, May 21). Maslow's hierarchy of needs. Retrieved from https://www.simplypsychology.org/maslow.html

Melendez, S. (2018, September 17). 4 sobering predictions about the future of jobs in an automated world. Retrieved October 3, 2019, from https://www.fastcompany.com/90237950/4-sobering-predictions- about-the-future-of-jobs-in-an-automated-world

Meyer, A., Rose, D., & Gordon, D. (2014,). *Universal Design for Learning: theory and practice.* Wakefield, MA: CAST.

Michel, K. (2014). Maslow's Hierarchy Connected to Blackfoot Beliefs. Retrieved March 10, 2019, from http://bit.ly/maslow-blackfoot-connection

Mitsuhashi, Y. (2017). A Japanese Concept to Improve Work and Life. Retrieved September 29, 2019, from https://www.bbc.com/worklife/article/20170807-ikigai-a-japanese-concept-to-improve-work-and-life

Murray, T. (2019) *Personal & Authentic: Designing learning experiences that impact a lifetime.* San Diego, CA IMPress, a division of Dave Burgess Consulting, Inc.

Pasricha, N. (2016, September 6). Why North Americans should consider dumping age-old retirement. Retrieved September 30, 2019, from https://www.thestar.com/life/relationships/2016/09/06/why-north-americans-should-consider-dumping-age-old-retirement-pasricha.html

Portnoy, L. (2019). *Designed to Learn: Using design thinking to bring purpose and passion to the classroom.* Alexandria, VA: ASCD.

Rath, T. (2007). *StrengthsFinder.* New York, NY: Gallup Press.

Rickabaugh, J. (2016). *Tapping the Power of Personalized Learning: A roadmap for school leaders.* Alexandria, VA: ASCD.

Robinson, K., & Aronica, L. (2014). *Finding your element: how to discover your talents and passions and transform your life.* London: Penguin Books.

Rouquet, T., & Hausermann, L. (2017, February 25). The 4 industrial revolutions. Retrieved September 19, 2019, from https://www.sentryo.net/the-4-industrial-revolutions/

Serveyev, A. (2019). 16 Important Signs You Are Heading for Burnout. Retrieved September 29, 2019, from http://timewiser.com/blog/16-important-signs-you-are-heading-for-burnout/

Sinek, S. (2009). *Start with Why: How great leaders inspire everyone to take action.* New York, NY: Penguin Group (USA) LLC.

Sinek, S., Mad, D., & Docker, P. (2017). *Find Your Why: A practical guide for discovering purpose for you and your team.* New York, NY: Portfolio/Penguin. An Imprint of Penguin Random House LLC.

Snyder, J. (2016, September 29). The Ticking Clock of Teacher Burnout. Retrieved September 29, 2019, from https://www.theatlantic.com/education/archive/2016/09/the-ticking-clock-of-us-teacher-burnout/502253/

Sone, T., Nakaya, N., Ohmori, K., Shimazu, T., Higashiguchi, M., Kakizaki, M., Kikuchi, N., & Kuriyama, S. (2008, July 7). Sense of life worth living (ikigai) and mortality in Japan: Ohsaki Study. Retrieved September 30, 2019 from https://www.ncbi.nlm.nih.gov/pubmed/18596247

Welcome, A. (2018). *Run Like a PIRATE: Push yourself to get more out of life.* San Diego, CA: Dave Burgess Consulting, Inc.

Wiskup, M. (2007). *The It Factor: Be the one people like, listen to, and remember.* AMACOM: New York, NY.

INDEX

ABOUT THE AUTHOR

About Barbara

Barbara Bray is a creative learning strategist who has been on a journey to transform teaching and learning for over thirty years. Barbara's story goes down multiple paths that helped her find what she is passionate about and fighting for. She grew up in Maryland in a creative household that encouraged curiosity. The school was different. The only way she would survive school was to be compliant because her first-grade teacher told her that. She was labeled a poor reader and a troublemaker, so she did school to get through school. Because her dad got a job in California, they moved the day after her high school graduation.

Barbara realized this move was a fresh start for her. No one knew her or her labels. She went to the community college and excelled in all her classes. Her counselor pointed her to the new dental hygiene program so she applied and was accepted. Then she got married, moved to their home in the Oakland hills, and had two amazing children. Barbara was able to work part-time, teach dental hygiene, and work at her children's school. It was during that time she was excited about computers and teaching. She took every class she could and ended up setting up and running a computer program for the school.

Then something happened. Barbara went to get her dog off the deck that was not finished and tripped and fell. When she came to, her leg was broken and her neck was damaged. This changed everything for her. When she recuperated, she had to quit dental hygiene and went back to school to become a teacher. She went from "dental flossing to mental flossing."

Barbara always encouraged curiosity and wonder in her classes and workshops. Through her work as a teacher, adjunct professor, instructional designer, speaker, and writer, she explored different pathways where she could make a difference in children's lives. Each opportunity led to the next and Barbara kept seeing that the connections she made at conferences and on social media helped her grow as a learner. She wrote a column for CUE, posted often on her blog, created My eCoach, a platform for teachers, and presented at conferences. She co-founded Personalize Learning, LLC and co-authored two books, Make Learning Personal and How to Personalize Learning with Kathleen McClaskey. Barbara eventually wanted to know more about the stories and the WHY. In 2017, Barbara started her Rethinking Learning podcast and is a co-host for the #rethink_learning Twitter chat. The stories she learned from others opened doors for her to the WHY over and over again.

This is her why for this book: *Define Your WHY*. She wasn't living her life on purpose until she told her story and listened to the stories of so many inspirational thought leaders. She has been keynoting and doing workshops on *Define Your WHY* for over three years and it was time to write about the stories and share the activities. All along

Barbara has been an advocate for educators to change the system so every learner had a voice and choice in their learning. Now she believes this book can help anyone who is searching to discover or rediscover their WHY so they can live and learn on purpose.

Barbara Bray, Creative Learning Strategist

Email: barbara.bray@gmail.com

Twitter: @bbray27 #defineyourWHY #rethink_learning

Website: https://barbarabray.net

OTHER EDUMATCH TITLES

WWW.EDUMATCHPUBLISHING.COM

Journey to The "Y" in You by Dene Gainey
This book started as a series of separate writing pieces that were eventually
woven together to form a fabric called The Y in You. The question is,
"What's the 'why' in you?"

The Fire Within
Compiled and edited by Mandy Froehlich
Adversity itself is not what defines us. It is how we react to that adversity and the choices we make that creates who we are and how we will persevere.

Stories of EduInfluence by Brent Coley
In Stories of EduInfluence, veteran educator Brent Coley shares stories from more than two decades in the classroom and front office.

In Other Words by Rachelle Dene Poth
In Other Words is a book full of inspirational and thought-provoking quotes that have pushed the author's thinking and inspired her.

One Drop of Kindness by Jeff Kubiak
This children's book, along with each of you, will change our world as we know it. It only takes One Drop of Kindness to fill a heart with love.

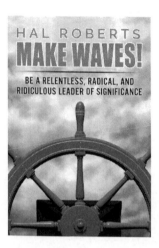

Make Waves! by Hal Roberts
In Make Waves! Hal discusses 15 attributes of a great leader. He shares his varied experience as a teacher, leader, a player in the N.F.L., and a plethora of research to take you on a journey to emerge as leader of significance.

Unconventional by Rachelle Dene Poth
Unconventional will empower educators to take risks, explore new ideas and emerging technologies, and bring amazing changes to classrooms. Dive in to transform student learning and thrive in edu!

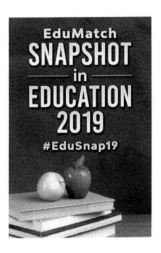

EduMatch Snapshot in Education 2019
EDive in as an international crew of educators share a snapshot of what they learned, what they did, and how they grew in 2019. Topics include Social Emotional Learning, identity, instructional tips, and much more!

Strive by Rob Dunlop
This book will get you thinking about how happy you are in your career and give you practical strategies to make changes that will truly impact your happiness.

EduMatch Publishing

Made in the USA
San Bernardino, CA
20 March 2020